le

knit & wrap

NOTATION
PLAN

knit & wrap

25 capelets, cowls & collars

Nathalie Mornu

APPLE

First published in the UK in 2011 by
Apple Press
7 Greenland Street
London
www.apple-press.com

10 9 8 7 6 5 4 3 2 1

First Edition

Published by Lark Books in the USA
A Division of Sterling Publishing Co., Inc.
387 Park Avenue South, New York, NY 10016

ISBN: 978-1-84543-403-8
Manufactured in China

TECHNICAL EDITOR
Rita Greenfeder

PHOTOGRAPHY DIRECTOR
Dana Irwin

PHOTOGRAPHER
Lynne Harty

COVER DESIGNER
Chris Bryant

ART DIRECTOR
Kristi Pfeffer

INTERIOR DESIGNER
Pamela Norman

EDITORIAL ASSISTANT
Kathleen McCafferty

ILLUSTRATOR
Orrin Lundgren

contents

capelets

impulse wink coo enchanting tease | captivating charm coquette

CAPELETS float and flutter about the shoulders. They exude sophistication. Wear one, and you'll want to shrug or flounce to accentuate every point you make. Capelets say, yes, I'm modern, but I know when the tailors of yore had a great thing going, and I'm getting some of it for myself.

Most ponchos, they just don't have the same panache. Don't know why. Maybe it's their shape and length, which draws the eye away from a gorgeous face? Maybe it's the childish fringe. At any rate, it raises a question: What's the difference between a poncho and a capelet? Simple: Capes fasten at the neck (creating the opportunity to use gor-geous buttons or sinfully lavish ribbons), while ponchos don't. And capelets are merely shorter versions of capes.

Everyone knows that with the rules under your belt, you're free to break them. So while this section contains the sweet-est wisp of a capelet (page 22), a spectacular cabled number with an antique brooch closure (page 34), and a fairy tale showstopper with ribbons galore (page 38), you'll see that some of these capelet projects don't stick strictly to the definition. Bet you won't mind that one (page 14) has teeny capped sleeves or that another (page 18) slips on over the head.

Made with doubled chunky yarn, this capelet knits up in less time than it takes to blow someone a kiss (ok, well almost).

COO

design by **ELLA AVERBUKH**

SKILL LEVEL
Easy

FINISHED MEASUREMENTS
25.5 x 58cm / 10 x 23"

MATERIALS + TOOLS
- Patons Up Country (100% wool; 99g/ 3.5oz= 71m/78yds): (A) 1 skein, color Brown—approx 71m/78yds of extra chunky-weight yarn

- Noro Koreyon (100% wool; 50g/1.75oz= 99m/108yds): (B) ½ skein, color variegated brown—approx 54yds/50m of extra chunky-weight yarn
- Knitting needles: 9mm (size 13 U.S.) and 15mm (size 19 U.S.) or size to obtain gauge
- 1 button, 3cm/1" in diameter
- Tapestry needle

GAUGE
- 3 sts = 10cm/4" worked on 15mm (size 19 U.S.) needles in Rib st
- *Always take time to check your gauge.*

Instructions

Neckband

With smaller needles and A, cast on 31 sts.
Purl 5 rows.
Cast off all sts.

Stand-Up Collar

Note Use the last loop (st) that remains on the last row cast-off st of the neckband as 1st st when picking up sts along one long side of the neckband.

Row 1 With RS facing, using larger needles and B, pick up 31 sts evenly along one long side of neckband.
Row 2 (WS) K1, *p1, k1; rep from * across.
Row 3 (RS) P1, *k1, p1; rep from * across.
Cast off all sts.

Connect the yarn along the shorter side of the top fringe, going down along the short side of the neckband. It is now on the bottom of the neckband.

Shoulder Capelet

Note Use the last loop (st) that remains from weaving in the yarn from the stand-up collar to the neckband when picking up the sts on the bottom long side of the neckband.

Row 1 With the RS facing, using larger needles and B, pick up 31 sts evenly along other long side of neckband.
Row 2 (WS) P1, *k1, p1; rep from * across.
Row 3 K1, *p1, k1-f/b; rep from * across, end k1.
Row 4 P1, *k1, p2; rep from * across, end k1, p1.
Row 5 K1, *p1, k2; rep from * across, end p1, k1.
Row 6 Rep Row 4.
Row 7 Cast off.

Finish

Sew button on neckband. Weave in yarn ends.

VARIATION

Because the stitches are so large, you can fasten into almost any spot you like. Loop the button into the collar for the raffish look shown here; if you prefer to go more buttoned up, fasten into the neckband instead.

wink

Look carefully, because it's subtle, and you'll notice the cables on this cute little number are shaped like owls, with buttons for eyes.

design by **BETSY FARQUHAR**

SKILL LEVEL
Intermediate

FINISHED MEASUREMENTS
Chest 86.5 (99, 110.5, 122)cm /
34 (39, 43½, 48)"

MATERIALS + TOOLS
- Blue Sky Alpaca Bulky (50% alpaca, 50% wool; 100g /3.5oz = 41m/45yd): 4 (5, 6, 7) skeins, color Polar Bear #1004—approx 165 (206, 247, 288)m/180 (225, 270, 315) yds of extra chunky-weight yarn
- Knitting needles: 9mm (size 13 U.S.) straight or 81cm/32" long circular needles; 4 double-pointed needles or size to obtain gauge
- Cable needle
- One hook-and-eye closure
- 16 buttons, 13mm/½" in diameter
- Embroidery thread
- Sewing needle
- Tapestry needle

GAUGE
- 8 sts/10 rows = 10cm/4" worked on 9mm (size 13 U.S.) needles in Pattern st
- *Always take time to check your gauge.*

SPECIAL ABBREVIATIONS
- **C4B** Place the first 2 sts on cn, hold in back of work, k2, then k2 from cn.
- **C4F** Place the first 2 sts on cn, hold in front of work, k2, then k2 from cn.
- **C4BP** Place the first 2 sts on cn, hold in back of work, k2, then p2 from cn.
- **C4FP** Place the first 2 sts on cn, hold in front of work, p2, then k2 from the cn.

PATTERN STITCHES

■ Pattern A

Row 1 (RS) K1, p1, k to within last 2 sts, p1, k1.

Row 2 (WS) K2, p to within last 2 sts, k2. Rep Rows 1 and 2, working center sts in St st with a vertical rib on ends, which keeps edges from rolling.

■ Pattern B

Row 1 (RS) P1, k1, work row as indicated to last 2 sts, k1, p1.

Row 2 (WS) K1, p1, work row as indicated to last 2 sts, p1, k1.

Rep Rows 1 and 2, which is basically an inversion of Pattern A, serves the same function, and is used with the cable patt.

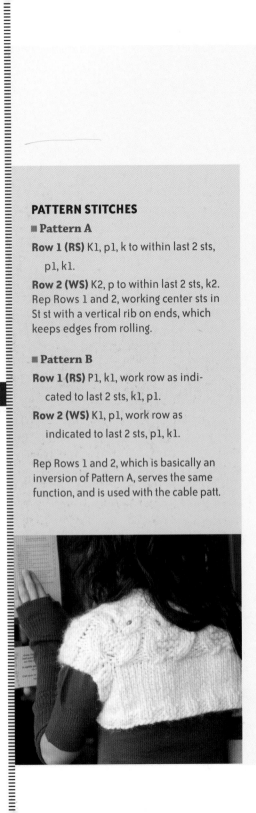

Instructions

Body

Cast on 78 (88, 98, 108) sts.

Work in k2, p2 rib for 3 rows.

Work in Pattern A for 7 rows.

Short Row Work first 59 (61, 63, 65) sts in Pattern A, wrap and turn, k40 (42, 44, 46), wrap and turn, p to end, working last 2 sts in Pattern A.

Armhole Openings

Cast-off Row (RS) Work 14 (16, 18, 20) sts in Pattern A, cast off next 10 (12, 14, 16) sts, k30 (32, 34, 36) center sts, cast off 10 (12, 14, 16) sts, work last 14 (16, 18, 20) sts in Pattern A—58 (64, 70, 76) sts.

Cast-on Row (WS) Work 14 (16, 18, 20) sts in Pattern A, cast on 12 (14, 16, 18) sts, p 30 (32, 34, 36) center sts, cast on 12 (14, 16, 18) sts, work last 14 (16, 18, 20) sts in Pattern A—82 (92, 102, 112) sts.

Next Row (RS) Work first 2 sts in Pattern A, p78 (88, 98, 108) sts, work last 2 sts in Pattern A.

Cable Panel

Note (Cable beg on a WS row.)

Next Row (WS) Work 2 sts in Pattern B, k3 (4, 5, 6), *follow cable chart, k1 (2, 3, 4); rep from * to last 5 (6, 7, 8) sts, k3 (4, 5, 6), work last 2 sts in Pattern B.

■ **KEY**

| G | **Garter: k on both** |

| I | **K on RS, p on WS** |

| • | **P on RS, k on WS** |

C4FP (*see Special Abbreviations*)

C4BP

C4F

C4B

■ **CABLE CHART**

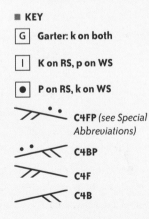

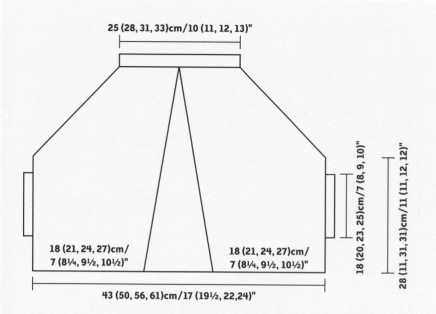

25 (28, 31, 33)cm/10 (11, 12, 13)"

18 (21, 24, 27)cm/
7 (8¼, 9½, 10½)"

18 (21, 24, 27)cm/
7 (8¼, 9½, 10½)"

18 (20, 23, 25)cm/7 (8, 9, 10)"

28 (11, 31, 31)cm/11 (11, 12, 12)"

43 (50, 56, 61)cm/17 (19½, 22,24)"

Next Row (RS) Work 2 sts in Pattern B, p3
(4, 5, 6), *follow cable chart, p1 (2, 3, 4);
rep * to last 5 (6, 7, 8) sts, p3 (4, 5, 6),
work last 2 sts in Pattern B.
Rep these 2 rows 7 times until 14 (16, 18,
20) rows are completed. **Note** You will
have 8 owls worked.

Next Row (WS) Work 2 sts in Pattern A, k78
(88, 98, 108), work last 2 sts in Pattern A.

Dec Rows

Row 1 (RS) Work 2 sts in Pattern A, k0 (2,
1, 0), (k2tog, k1) to within last 2 (4, 3,
2) sts, k0 (2, 1, 0), work 2 sts in Pattern
A—56 (64, 70, 76) sts.

Row 2 (WS) Work in Pattern A.

Row 3 Work 2 sts in Pattern A, k2 (0, 0, 0),
(k2tog, k1) to within last 4 (2, 2, 2) sts,
k2 (0, 0, 0), work 2 sts in Pattern A—40

(44, 48, 52) sts.

Row 4 Rep Row 2.

Neckline Ribbing

Work 3 (3, 5, 5) rows more in k2, p2 rib.
Cast off in rib.

Finish

With RS of sleeve facing you and using
dpns, starting at the center bottom of the
armhole, pick up 28 (32, 36, 40) sts evenly
all around the opening.

Join and work around in k2, p2 rib
for 3 (3, 7, 5) rnds.

Cast off in rib. Work the other sleeve the
same way. Using a tapestry needle, weave
in the ends. Using the sewing needle,
attach the hook-and-eye at the neck edge.
On each owl, sew on 2 buttons for eyes.

TIP
Different types of buttons, as well as
their positioning on the face, will give
the owls different expressions. The
version shown uses 2-hole buttons.

You just can't help it—you hug people you hardly know, kiss on the first date, and get lost in the excitement of your crushes.

impulse

design by **ELLA AVERBUKH**

SKILL LEVEL
Easy

FINISHED MEASUREMENTS
30cm/12" wide; 107cm/42" in circumference

MATERIALS + TOOLS
- Lion Brand Fettuccini (45% wool, 45% acrylic, 10% wool; 50g/1.75oz= 30m/33yd): (A) 2 skeins, color Twilight—approx 60m/66yds of extra chunky-weight yarn
- Patons Up Country (100% wool; 100g/3.5oz= 71m/78yds): (B) 1 skein, color Deep Steel Blue—approx 71m/78yds of extra chunky-weight yarn
- Knitting needles: 25mm (size 50 U.S.) or size needed to obtain gauge
- Cable needle
- Tapestry needle

GAUGE
- $3\frac{1}{2}$ sts = 10cm/4" worked on 25mm (size 50 U.S.) needles in St st
- *Always take time to check your gauge.*

SPECIAL ABBREVIATIONS
- **C6F** Place 3 sts onto cn and hold in front, k3, then k3 from cn.

Instructions

With one strand each of A and B held tog, cast on 10 sts.

Row 1 (WS) P1, k1, p6, k1, p1.

Row 2 (RS) K1, p1, k6, p1, k1.

Row 3 (WS) P1, k1, p6, k1, p1.

Rows 4–9 Rep Rows 2 and 3 for 6 rows.

Row 10 (RS) K1, p1, C6F, p1, k1.

Row 11 P1, k1, p6, k1, p1.

Row 12 K1, p1, k6, p1, k1.

Rows 13–20 Rep Row 11 and 12 for 8 rows.

Cast off.

Finish

Use last loop (st) rem from closing last row of Front of Wrap as first st when casting on connecting sts on both sides (A and B) of Front Piece.

Connect top corners (of A and B) of Front Piece with loop.

Cast on 1 st on 2nd row st of Side B— 2 sts on needle.

K1, p1, then connect 1 st on 3rd row side A—3 sts on needle.

P1, k1, p1, then connect 1 st on 4th row side B—4 sts on needle.

Cont in this manner until 10 rows of Sides A and B are connected.

Cast off. Weave in yarn ends.

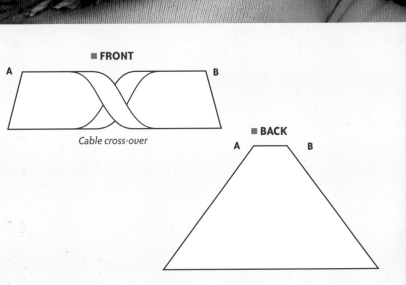

■ **FRONT**

A   B

Cable cross-over

■ **BACK**

A   B

The photos
say it all—
need we add
more?

enchanting

design by **SIOBHAN BROWN**

SKILL LEVEL
Intermediate

FINISHED MEASUREMENTS
23 x 48cm/9 x 19"

MATERIALS + TOOLS
- Sirdar Big Softie (51%wool, 49% acrylic; 50g/1.75oz= 45m/49yds): 1 ball, color Kitten #338—approx 45m/49yds of extra chunky-weight yarn
- Knitting needles: 10mm (size 15 U.S.) or size to obtain gauge
- 102cm/40" of black velvet ribbon
- Large sewing needle or tapestry needle

GAUGE
- 9 sts/12 rows = 10cm/4" worked on 10mm (size 15 U.S.) needles in pattern.
- *Always take time to check your gauge.*

Instructions
Cast on 43 sts.

Row 1 (RS) K1tbl, *p1, p1tbl, k1tbl; rep from * across.

Row 2 (WS) P1tbl, *k1tbl, k1, p1tbl; rep from * across.

Rows 3–10 Rep Rows 1 and 2 four more times.

Row 11 (RS) K1tbl, *drop next st off left needle, p1tbl, k1tbl; rep from * across.

Row 12 (WS) P1tbl, *k1tbl, p1tbl; rep from * across.

Row 13 (RS) K1tbl, *p1tbl, k1tbl; rep from * across.

Rows 14–16 Rep Rows 12 and 13 once more, then Row 12 once.
Cast off in k1, p1 rib.

Finish
Locate the first st you dropped and tease apart all the sts below it so that they form a loose ladder. Do this for each dropped st, including the cast-on edge. Sew in the two ends of the yarn. Thread the ribbon at regular intervals through the rib sts at the neck edge of the capelet. Weave in yarn ends.

Spin your spell *and* stay warm in this arresting hooded capelet.

design by **ELLA AVERBUKH**

tease

SKILL LEVEL

Intermediate

FINISHED MEASUREMENTS

51cm/20" around neck; 76cm/30" total length

MATERIALS + TOOLS

- Patons Up Country (100% wool; 100g/3.5oz= 71m/78yds): 2 skeins, color Charcoal #80996—approx 143m/156ydsof extra chunky-weight yarn
- Knitting needles: 15mm (size 19 U.S.) or size to obtain gauge
- Cable needle
- 1 button, 3.5 cm (1⅜") in diameter
- 1 button, 1.6 cm (⅝") in diameter
- Tapestry needle

GAUGE

- 12 sts = 10cm/4" worked on 15mm (size 19 U.S.) needles in St st
- *Always take time to check your gauge.*

SPECIAL ABBREVIATIONS

- **5-st front cable** Sl 2 sts to cn and hold in front, sl 1 p st and hold in back, k2, p1 from cn, k2 from cn).
- **6-st front cable** Sl 2 sts to cn and hold in front, sl 2 p sts and hold in back, k2, p2 from cn, k2 from cn.

Instructions

Horizontal Neck Cable

Cast on 9 sts.

Row 1 (RS) P2, k2, p1, k2, p2.

Row 2 (WS) K2, p2, k1, p2, k2.

Rows 3–4 Rep Rows 1 and 2 once.

Row 5 (RS) P2, 5-st front cable, p2.

Row 6 (WS) K2, p2, k1, p2, k2.

Rows 7–12 Rep Rows 1 and 2 three times.

Rows 13–36 Rep Rows 5–12 three
more times.

Rows 37–42 Rep Rows 5–10.
Cast off 9 sts.

Shoulder Capelet

Note Use the last loop (st) remaining on
the last cast-off st of the Horizontal Neck
Cable as the 1st st when picking the sts
along one long side of the Horizontal
Neck Cable.

Row 1 With RS facing, pick up 25 sts
evenly along one long side of Horizontal
Neck Cable.

Row 2 (WS) P1, *k1, p1; rep from across
row.

Row 3 (RS) K1, *p1, k1-f/b; rep from *
across row, end p1, k1.

Row 4 (WS) P1, *k1-f/b, p2; rep from *
across row, end k1-f/b, p1.

Row 5 (RS) K1, *p2, k2; rep from * across
row, end, p2, k1.

Row 6 (WS) P1, *k2, p2; rep from * across
row, end k2, p1.

Row 7 (RS) K1, *p2, 6-st front cable*, rep
from * to * once, (p2, k2) rib to last 17 sts,
(6-st front cable, p2) twice, k1.

Row 8 Rep Row 6.

Row 9 Rep Row 5.

Rows 10–14 Rep Rows 6 and 5 two
times more. Cast off all sts on row.

Hood

With RS facing, pick up 29 sts evenly
along other long side of the Horizontal
Neck Cable.

Row 1 (WS) K1, *p1, k1; rep from * across.

Row 2 (RS) Maintain est rib working first 2
and last 2 sts tog.

Rows 3–6 Rep Row 2 every other row
4 more times—17 sts.

Row 7 (WS) Work in est rib.

Row 8 (RS) K1, *k1-f/b, p1; rep from *
across row, end k1-f/b, k1.

Row 9 P3, *k1-f/b, p2; rep from * across
row, end p1.

Row 10 K3, *p2, k1-f/b, k1; rep from *
across row, end p2, k3.

Row 11 P3, *k2, p3; rep from * across row.

Row 12 K3, *p2, k3; rep from * across row.

Rows 13–22 Rep Rows 11 and 23 for 10
more rows.

Row 23 K1, k2tog, *p2tog, k1, k2tog; rep
from * across row, k2tog, k1.

Row 24 P2, k1, *p2tog, k1; rep from *
across row, end p2.

Row 25 K1, p1 (k1, p1, k1) tog as a k st,
(p1, k1, p1) tog as a p st to last st, k1.

Row 26 P1, (k1, p1, k1) tog as k st, (p1, k1,
p1) tog as p st.

Rep Rows 25 and 26 until about 5 sts rem.
Cast off the rem sts.

Finish

Weave in ends. Sew the button at
the neck.

A lacy capelet
like this one may
look demure...but
you sure don't
have to act that way.
Go on—be sassy
and flirtatious.

captivating

design by **ELIZABETH LOVICK**

SKILL LEVEL
Intermediate

FINISHED MEASUREMENTS
15cm/6" wide x 41 (46, 51)cm/
16 (18, 20)" circumference

MATERIALS + TOOLS
- ColourMart 2/14NM Cashmere
  (100% 4-ply cashmere; 150g/5¼oz
  = 1052m/1150yds): 35 (40, 45)g, color
  Black—approx 347 (438, 530)m/380
  (480, 580)yds of lace-weight yarn
- Knitting needles: 3.75mm (size 5 U.S.)
  or size to obtain gauge; 3.25mm (size 3
  U.S.) needle for picking up stitches
- Cable needle
- Tapestry needle
- Row counter
- 8 (9, 10) stitch markers
- Small stitch holder
- 5 buttons, 13mm/½" in diameter

GAUGE
- 23 sts = 10cm/4" worked on 3.75mm
  (size 5 U.S.) needles over the neck frill
  pattern after washing and blocking
- *Always take time to check your gauge.*

SPECIAL ABBREVIATIONS
- **SM** Slip Marker
- **C6B** Place 3 sts on cn, hold in back of
  the work, k3, then k3 sts from cn.
- **C6F** Place 3 sts on cn, hold in front of
  the work, k3, then k3 sts from cn.

NOTES

■ Stitch markers are not mentioned unless they're important. When they aren't mentioned, slip them when you come to them.

■ The cable section is worked first, using 2 strands of yarn. The sts are picked up along one side of the cable for the Neck Frill, which is worked with one strand of yarn. The sts are then picked up along the other edge of the cable and the Collar is worked using a single strand. Sts are then picked up along the 2 ends of the Collar and Cable panels and the button and buttonhole bands are worked lengthwise.

Instructions

Cable Band

Using 3.75mm (size 5 U.S.) needles and 2 strands of yarn held together, cast on 13 sts.

Row 1 (RS) P2, k9, p2.

Row 2 and all even rows K2, p9, k2.

Row 3 P2, k3 C6B, p2.

Row 5 Rep Row 1.

Row 7 P2, C6F, k3, p2.

Row 8 Rep Row 2.

Rows 9–136 (152, 168) Rep Rows 1–8, 16 (18, 20) times more.

Break yarn, place sts on a thread. They will be picked up later when working the buttonhole band.

Neck Frill

With RS facing and using 3.25mm (size 3 U.S.) needle and one strand of yarn, pick up and k123 (135, 147) sts along one edge of Cable Band.

Change to 3.75mm (size 5 U.S.) needles and work as foll:

Set up row (WS) K2, p to last 2 sts, k2.

Row 1 K1, *k1, yo, k1, k3tog, k1, yo; rep from * to last 2 sts, k2.

Row 2 K2, p to last 2 sts, k2.

Rows 3–6 Rep Rows 1 and 2 twice more.

Row 7 Rep Row 1.

■ **KEY**

 C6F

 C6B

☐ K on RS rows, p on WS rows

⋏ K3tog

⧅ SsK

⧄ K2tog

○ YO

● P on RS rows, K on WS rows

☐ No stitch

■ **CABLE BAND**

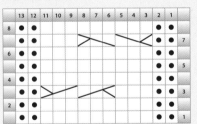

■ **NECK FRILL**

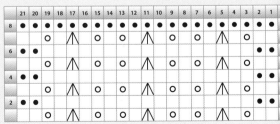

Row 8 Knit.

Row 9 Cast off pwise.

Shoulder Capelet

(chart appears on page 32)

With RS facing and size 3.25mm (size 3 U.S) needles and one strand of yarn, pick up and k81 (91, 101) sts along other edge of Cable Panel.

Change to 3.75 mm (size 5 U.S.) needles.

Next Row P1, *PM, p10; rep from * to end of row.

Row 1 *K1, yo, k1, yo, k2, k3tog, k2, yo, k1, yo, SM; rep from * to last st, k1.

Row 2 and all even rows Purl.

Row 3 *K2, yo, k3, k3tog, k3, yo, k1, SM; rep from * to last st, k1.

Row 5 *K1, yo, k2, yo, k2, k3tog, k2, yo, k2, yo, SM; rep from * to last st, k1.

Row 7 *K1, k2tog, yo, k2, yo, k1, k3tog, k1, yo, k2, yo, ssk, SM; rep from * to last st, k1.

Row 9 *K1, yo, k2tog, yo, k3, yo, k3tog, yo, k3, yo, ssk, yo, SM; rep from * to last st, k1.

Row 11 *K2, k2tog, yo, k3, yo, k3tog, yo, k3, yo, ssk, k1, SM; rep from * to last st, k1.

Row 13 *K1, yo, k1, k2tog, yo, k3, yo, k3tog, yo, k3, yo, ssk, k1, yo, SM; rep from * to last st, k1.

32

■ SHOULDER CAPELET CHART

| | 30 | 29 | 28 | 27 | 26 | 25 | 24 | 23 | 22 | 21 | 20 | 19 | 18 | 17 | 16 | 15 | 14 | 13 | 12 | 11 | 10 | 9 | 8 | 7 | 6 | 5 | 4 | 3 | 2 | 1 | |

■ **KEY** *Note that each row finishes with an extra k1.*

	No stitch		/𝗜\	K3tog
	K on RS rows, p on WS rows		\	Ssk
o	YO		/	K2tog

Row 15 *K3, k2tog, yo, k3, yo, k3tog, yo, k3, yo, ssk, k2, SM; rep from * to last st, k1.

Row 17 *K1, yo, k2, k2tog, yo, k3, yo, k3tog, yo, k3, yo, ssk, k2, yo, SM; rep from * to last st, k1.

Row 19 *K6, yo, ssk, k1, yo, k3tog, yo, k1, k2tog, yo, k5, SM; rep from * to last st, k1.

Row 21 *K1, yo, k2, k2tog, yo, k2, yo, ssk, yo, k3tog, yo, k2tog, yo, k2, yo, ssk, k2, yo, SM; rep from * to last st, k1.

Row 23 *K3, k2tog, yo, k1, yo, ssk, k1, yo, ssk, k1, k2tog, yo, k1, k2tog, yo, k1, yo, ssk, k2, SM; rep from * to last st, k1.

Row 25 *K1, yo, k1, k2tog, yo, k3, yo, ssk, k1, yo, k3tog, yo, k1, k2tog, yo, k3, yo, ssk, k1, yo, SM; rep from * to last st, k1.

Row 27 *K2, k2tog, yo, k5, yo, ssk, k3, k2tog, yo, k5, yo, ssk, k1, SM; rep from * to last st, k1.

Row 29 *K1, yo, k2tog, yo, k7, yo, ssk, k1, k2tog, yo, k7, yo, ssk, yo, SM; rep from * to last st, k1.

Row 31 *K1, yo, k2tog, yo, [k3, yo, k3tog, yo] 3 times, k3, yo, ssk, yo, SM; rep from * to last st, k1.

Row 33 *K1, yo, k2tog, yo, K1, [k3, yo, k3tog, yo] 3 times, k4, yo, ssk, yo, SM; rep from * to last st, k1.

Row 35 *K1, yo, k1, k3tog, k1, yo; rep from * to last st, k1.

Rows 37, 39, 41, and 43 Rep Row 35.
Row 44 Knit.
Row 45 Cast off pwise.

Button Band

With RS facing and size 3.25mm (size 3 U.S.) needle and one strand of yarn, pick up and k 44 sts along the left front edge, including Cable Band sts but excluding the Neck Frill.
  Change to 3.75mm (size 5 U.S. needles).
  Knit 9 rows.
  Cast off kwise.

Buttonhole Band

With RS facing and size 3.25mm (size 3 U.S.) needles and one strand of yarn, pick up and k 44 sts along the right front edge, including Cable Band sts but excluding the Neck Frill.

Change to 3.75mm (size 5 U.S. needles).
  Knit 4 rows.

Buttonhole Row K5, *k2tog, yo, k6; rep from * four times, end k2tog, yo, k5.
  K 4 rows.
  Cast off kwise.

Finish

Weave in all ends but don't cut them. Wash and towel dry the piece. Block the collar on a flat surface. Pin the low edge of the Cable Band into a circle, then pin the Shoulder Capelet, pinning each point of the outer edge to form the peaks. Finally, pin the front edges.

Allow the Neck Frill to stand upright, putting pins behind it if necessary to support it. Pull each point of the neck frill up to form the peaks. Rep this as necessary during the drying process.

When dry, cut off the yarn ends. Sew on the buttons.

Proper Victorian capelet?
Depends on how you
rock it. Wear it with
jeans, stilettos, and a
décolleté down to here,
and people will be calling
the fire department.

design by **TANYA WADE**

charm

SKILL LEVEL
Intermediate

FINISHED MEASUREMENTS
48cm/19" wide at collar; 127cm/50" wide at base; 38cm/15" from top to bottom

MATERIALS + TOOLS
- Debbie Bliss Como (50% merino wool, 50% cashmere; 49g/1.75oz= 42m/46yds): 9 balls, color Gray #2—approx 379m/414yds of extra chunky-weight yarn
- Knitting needles: 10mm (size 15 U.S.) 91cm/36" circular needles or size needed to obtain gauge
- Cable needle
- 2 removable markers
- Tapestry needle
- Link chain, 89cm/35" long
- 1 brooch

GAUGE
- 8 sts/14 rows = 10cm/4" worked on 10mm (size 15 U.S.) needles in pattern
- *Always take time to check your gauge.*

SPECIAL ABBREVIATIONS
- **C6F** Place 3 sts onto cn and hold to front of work, k3, then k3 from cn.
- **SM** Slip marker
- **C6B** Place 3 sts onto cn and hold to back of work, k3, then k3 from cn.

Instructions

Using 10mm (size 15 U.S.) needles, cast on 154 sts. Work 5 rows in Garter st (page 104).

Row 1 (RS): K5, PM, k144, PM, k5.

Note Keep first 5 and last 5 sts in Garter st until decs.

Row 2 and all WS rows K5, SM, p144, SM, k5.

Row 3 K5, SM, *k6, C6F; rep from *, SM, k5.

Row 4 Rep Row 2.

Row 5 Knit all sts.

Row 6 Rep Row 2.

Row 7 K5, SM, *C6B, k6; rep from *, SM, k5.

Row 8 Rep Row 2.

Row 9 Knit all sts.

Row 10 Rep Row 2.

Row 11 K5, SM, *k2tog, k4, C6F; rep from *, SM, k5—142 sts.

Row 12 Rep Row 2.

Row 13 K5, SM, k132, SM, k5.

Row 14 Rep Row 2.

Row 15 K5, SM, *C6B, k5; rep from *, SM, k5.

Row 16 Rep Row 2.

Row 17 Knit all sts.

Row 18 Rep Row 2.

Row 19 K5, SM, *k2tog, k3, C6F; rep from *, SM, k5—130 sts.

Row 20 Rep Row 2.

Row 21 Knit all sts.

Row 22 Rep Row 2.

Row 23 K5, SM, *C6B, k4; rep from *, SM, k5.

Row 24 Rep Row 2.

Row 25 Knit all sts.

Row 26 Rep Row 2.

Row 27 K5, SM, *k2tog, k2, C6F; rep from *, SM, k5—118 sts.

Row 28 Rep Row 2.

Row 29 Knit all sts.

Row 30 Rep Row 2.

Row 31 K5, SM, *C6B, k3; rep from *, SM, k5.

Row 32 Rep Row 2.

Row 33 Knit all sts.

Row 34 Rep Row 2.

Row 35 K5, SM, * k2tog, k1, C6F; rep from *, SM, k5—106 sts.

Row 36 Rep Row 2.

Row 37 Knit all sts.

Row 38 Rep Row 2.

Row 39 K5, SM, C6F, k2; rep from, SM, k5.

Row 40 Rep Row 2.

Collar decs beg

Row 41 K4tog, *k2, k2tog; rep from * to last

6 sts, k2, k4tog tbl—76 sts.

Row 42 P2, p2tog tbl, p2, p2tog tbl, p to last 8 sts, p2tog, p2, p2tog, p2—72 sts.

Collar

Row 43 K3, *C6F; rep from * to last 3 sts, k3.

Row 44 Purl all sts.

Row 45 Knit all sts.

Row 46 Purl all sts.

Row 47 *C6B; rep to end.

Row 48 Purl all sts.

Row 49 Knit all sts.

Row 50 Purl all sts.

Row 51 K3, *C6F; rep from * to last 3 sts, k3.

Row 52 Purl all sts.

Row 53 Knit all sts.

Row 54 Cast off all sts pwise.

Finish

Weave in yarn ends.

Thread the chain through the openings in 1st row made from Basketweave Cable. To wear the capelet closed, open the brooch and slide the pin through both end links of the chain, then close the brooch. Alternately, you can eliminate the chain closure and simply close the capelet with a brooch.

In this beribboned confection, people may mistake you for one of Marie-Antoinette's *demoiselles*. Just bat your eyelashes and tell them, *"Mais non."*

design by **BETH TODD**

coquette

SKILL LEVEL
Easy

FINISHED MEASUREMENTS
102 x 28 cm/40 x 11" (before weaving in drawstring and ribbons)

MATERIALS + TOOLS
- Classic Elite Miracle (50% alpaca, 50% Tencel; 99g/3.5oz= 99m/108yds): 2 skeins, color Purple Palace #3354— approx 216yds/198m of aran-weight yarn
- Knitting needles: 5.5mm (size 9 U.S.) straight needles 36mm/14" long or size needed to obtain gauge
- Crochet hook 4mm (size G-6 U.S.)
- 30 coil-less safety pins
- Stitch markers, optional
- Ribbon or fabric for decorative strips (see box on page 43)
- Large-eyed tapestry needle or safety pin for weaving in fabric strips

GAUGE
- 15 sts/21 rows = 10cm/4" worked on 5.5mm (size 9 U.S.) needles in St st (before dropping sts)
- *Always take time to check your gauge.*

SPECIAL ABBREVIATIONS
- **k1tbl** k 1 through back loop.

NOTES

- It's essential to use the E-Wrap Loop cast on, which is explained at right. To make it easier to work the 1st row into the cast on, use 36mm/14" straight needles to cast on and knit the first row; then, if desired, switch to circular needles for the rest of the pattern.

- The first 4 and last 4 sts of each row form a Garter st edging and need to be worked in the back loop of each st. Place stitch markers after the first 4 sts and before the last 4 sts to help you remember to k into the back loop on every row.

- The ribbons will be woven in and out of the columns of ladders, formed from dropping sts after the capelet has been knitted. More detailed instructions are in the Finish section.

Instructions

E-Wrap Loop cast on

This cast on is called E-wrap or E-Loop because it resembles a series of cursive small-letter E's written in a continuous line across a page.

Leaving a 2.5–7.5cm/2–3" end tail, make a slipknot and place it on one of the knitting needles. Hold the needle in your RH, and with your LH open with palm facing you, lay the yarn coming from the needle across the left palm and then hold the needle behind your LH.

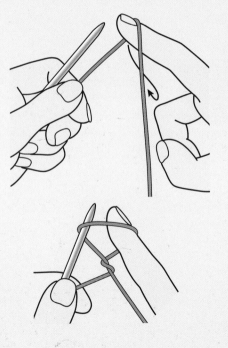

Close the fingers of the LH around the yarn, keeping the index finger pointing away from you, with the yarn draped over it. Turn your LH toward your RH and move the needle tip toward the left palm. Your left index finger and the needle should be at right angles. Move the needle tip and insert it under the yarn on your finger, from the bottom of your index finger moving toward the tip end of the finger. The yarn should now be wrapped around both needle and finger; remove the finger from the yarn loop and tighten the loop now on the needle by moving the LH holding the yarn away from your RH. You should now have 2 loops (sts) on the needle.

Continue in this manner, adding loops until you have 129 sts on the needle.

Capelet

Row 1 Knit each cast-on st. When knitting into a cast-on loop, it helps to loosen it up with your left thumb as you knit into it. Make sure to not pull the sts far apart as you work them off the left needle—129 sts.

Rows 2–5 K each of the 1st 4 sts tbl (k1tbl), k across to last 4 sts, k each into back loop—129 sts.

Row 6 (WS) (K1tbl) 4 sts, p across to last 4 sts, (k1tbl) 4 sts—129 sts.

Row 7 (RS) (K1tbl) 4 sts, k across to last 4 sts, (k1tbl) 4 sts—129 sts.

Rows 8–49 Rep Rows 6 and 7 another 21 times—129 sts.

Row 50 (WS) Rep Row 6—129 sts.

Row 51(RS) (K1tbl) 4 sts, drop next st off needle without knitting it and pin a coil-less safety pin onto the ladder formed after that st unravels, *k4 sts, drop next st and place pin as before, rep from * across to last 4 sts, (k1tbl) 4 sts—104 sts and 25 dropped sts.

Tip The coil-less pins will mark where to weave the drawstring cord through later.

Rows 52–56 For Garter St Band, (k1tbl) 4 sts, knit across to last 4 sts, (k1tbl) 4 sts—104 sts.

Row 57 (RS) Work 2 sts of elastic cast off (k1tbl), place these 2 sts back onto the left needle and k tog tbl [1 st bound off], (k1tbl the next st, place the 2 sts back onto left needle and k tog tbl) 2 times, *knit the next st, place the 2 sts onto left needle and k tog tbl, rep from * across to the last 4 sts, (k1tbl) the next st, place the 2 sts back onto left needle and (k tog tbl) 4 times. Fasten off yarn, and weave in the ends.

Unravel Dropped Sts

Holding the cast-off edge of the capelet in the LH, start unraveling one of the dropped sts by gently tugging right below the dropped st. After the loose st has traveled down for several rows, move your LH to grasp closer to the st, and pull your hands away from each other to loosen and unravel the sts further.

If the yarn tends to stick when unraveling the dropped sts, gently pull the sts apart on either side, then gently tug the top and bottom to release dropped st and get it to unravel.

There will be 25 columns of the dropped st ladders once all the dropped sts have been unraveled.

The hem may want to curl up and the remaining knit sts may spread out into the ladder openings made from the dropped sts. Don't worry: the hem won't curl up after weaving in the ribbons.

Drawstring Cord

Tip The flat drawstring cord won't twist as much if, at the end of each row, you alternate turning the work to the back and then next row turn to the front.

Using crochet hook, make a slipknot and place it on the hook. Ch 3, tr in 1st ch made, *ch 2, turn, tr into the space between the st and ch of the prev row, rep from * until length is about 165cm/65" or to the end of the yarn.

Fasten off. Weave in ends.

Use one of the coil-less safety pins attached to the end of the cord to carefully weave the drawstring cord in and out of the capelet from one side to the other side, just above the pin markers at the top of each dropped st column under the Garter St Band.

With the RS of the capelet facing you, insert the cord pin from the front to back in the top of the first ladder column in the space above the pin marker, then back to front through the top of next column. Continue weaving in this manner to the other side of the capelet. Center the drawstring cord in the capelet.

Note Due to the odd number of columns woven through, in order to get the drawstring ends positioned so they'll tie in the front of the capelet, the ends of the drawstring need to be woven between the last 2 sts of that row on each of the side edges. One cord end will exit out the front and the other will exit out the back.

Ribbons

Cut 12 strips 4cm/1½" wide and at least 64cm/25" long (see box on next page). For a really dramatic look, cut the strips longer than 76cm/30" to add extra length to both the fringes and bows. Fabric strips will tend to fray a bit, but that lends charm; it's not necessary to finish or hem the cut edges.

Weave the Ribbons

It's easier to weave in the ribbon if you fold the end in half lengthwise then thread the end of the ribbon into a large-eyed tapestry needle or attach a safety pin to it. Weave in the ribbons from the top down in the sequence of columns explained opposite. It's important to start in the same small space above the pin marker where the drawstring is also woven through. If you use 64cm/25"-long strips, leave about 26cm/10" at the top to tie into bows, so that approx 10cm/4" hangs below the bottom as fringe. For 76cm/30"-long strips, leave about 33cm/13" to tie into bows, with about 15cm/6" for the fringe.

With the RS of the capelet facing you, and starting at the top of the column just above the pin marker in the same space as the drawstring, weave under 2 ladders and over 2 ladders, alternating down to the last 5 ladders, then go over 1 and under 1 to the end.

Column 1 Weave ribbon

Column 2 Weave ribbon

Columns 3 and 4 Skip these columns

Columns 5 and 6 Weave ribbon

Columns 7–9 Skip

Columns 10 and 11 Weave ribbon

Columns 12–14 Skip

Columns 15 and 16 Weave ribbon

Columns 17–19 Skip

Columns 20 and 21 Weave ribbon

Colunns 22 and 23 Skip

Columns 24 and 25 Weave ribbon

Finish

After the ribbons have been woven, remove all the pins from the capelet. Tie the pairs of ribbons together into bows at the top of the capelet.

MATERIAL FOR DECORATIVE STRIPS

You can use anything you think is pretty for the decorative strips: ribbon, fabric, an old skirt, even a recycled T-shirt.

■ If you opt for ribbon, you'll need about 8m/8½ yd. Make sure it's 4cm/1½" wide.

■ To use fabric, get a square that's 51 x 76cm/20 x 30", or if you're simply buying it off the bolt, purchase 46cm/18". (This quantity yields exactly enough fabric to cut the 12 strips called for in the pattern. There's no room for error when cutting the strips, so be careful!)

■ Planning on cutting up an existing garment? Well, before you do, make sure you have enough material: do your math, and check it twice.

CUTTING DECORATIVE STRIPS FROM RECYCLED GARMENTS

To reuse a T-shirt or other piece of clothing, cut off and discard the hem before cutting the strips across the width of the shirt. If the garment has side seams, cut up one side-seam to make a flat piece, then slice the strips.

spellbound rapt dreamy — catch whisper crush sugar frivolous glances wis

cowls

COWLS nestle below the chin when they're small, and they're just adorable. But the voluminous ones sprawl out with a command: Look at me! You have to work these, baby, make 'em yours—drape them around the shoulders like you're a socialite; let them dangle, all relaxed like, from the neck; hide from view, snuggled deep inside; or play the diva by pulling an edge over your head like a hood.

The projects in this section get additional spice from awesome details. First, pompoms (pages 56 and 62)...who doesn't *love* them? Next, check out the off-kilter cables on page 60. You can't go wrong with frills—witness the bounty of delicate ruffles along the edges of the cowl on the page opposite. And bling-bling! Crystals sparkle in the folds of the project on page 54.

But okay, okay, restraint can be a great thing, too. The terrific project on page 72 is easy to make in Garter stitch and a delicious raspberry color.

This striking cowl comes in two versions: a smaller one and a larger version (shown here) for the daring fashion maverick.

spellbound

design by **ANET SKILLIN**
variation by **CHERYL WATERS**

Large Version

SKILL LEVEL
Easy

FINISHED MEASUREMENTS
- 86cm/34" long

MATERIALS + TOOLS
- Brown Sheep Burly Spun (100% wool; 400g/8oz= 119m/130yd): 3 skeins, color Aztec Turquoise #BS78— approx 390yds/356m of extra chunky-weight yarn
- Knitting needles: 19mm (size 35 U.S.) or size to obtain gauge
- 2 to 5 natural buttons, 4.5cm/1¾" in diameter
- Sewing needle
- Tapestry needle

GAUGE
- 6 sts/7¼ rows over 10cm/4" worked on 19 mm (size 35 U.S.) needles with two strands of yarn held together in St st
- *Always take time to check your gauge.*

NOTE
No buttonholes are necessary; since the stitches are so large, the buttons will slip easily through any of them, which gives the option of buttoning the cowl in several different ways.

Instructions

With 2 strands of yarn held tog, using
19 mm (size 35 U.S.) needles and long-tail
cast-on technique (page 103), cast on 28
sts. Work in k1, p1 ribbing for 86cm/34".

Cast off using sewn cast-off technique
(page 107).

Finish

If you're using more than 2 buttons, space
them evenly from edge to edge along the
cast-on end. For 2 buttons, place them
along the cast-on edge approximately
10cm/4" from each side. To stitch them
on, thread yarn through the buttons from
the front, and tie a knot on the back of
each button (this helps prevent them from
resting too tightly against the fabric).
Attach the buttons to the cowl. You might
opt to attach clear buttons to the back side
to help stabilize the button in the knitted
fabric.

Weave in yarn ends.

Small Version

SKILL LEVEL
Easy

FINISHED MEASUREMENTS
61cm/24" long

MATERIALS + TOOLS
- Debbie Bliss COMO (90% wool, 10% cashmere; 50g/1.75oz= 42m/46yd): 4 skeins, color Aqua #06—approx 168m/184yds of extra chunky-weight yarn
- Knitting needles: 25mm (size 50 U.S.) or size needed to obtain gauge
- 2 to 5 natural buttons, 4.5cm/1¾" in diameter
- Sewing needle
- Tapestry needle

GAUGE
- 5 sts/5 rows = 10 cm/4" worked on 25mm (size 50 U.S.) needles with 2 strands of yarn held together in St st
- *Always take time to check your gauge.*

NOTE
Buttonholes aren't necessary because the stitches are so large: buttons slip easily through them. This gives you the option of wearing the cowl in several different ways, depending on how you button it.

Instructions
With 2 strands of yarn held tog, using 25 mm (size 50 U.S.) needles and long-tail cast-on technique (page 103) cast on 28 sts. Work in k1, p1 ribbing for 86cm/34".

Cast off using a sewn cast-off (page 107).

Finish
Follow the instructions on page 48.

Vivid complementary colors knitted up in a bold graphic: what a knockout combination! All eyes are on you.

design by **BETSY FARQUHAR**

rapt

SKILL LEVEL
Intermediate

FINISHED MEASUREMENTS
30 x 28cm/12 x 11"

MATERIALS + TOOLS
- Reynolds Lopi (100% Icelandic wool; 100g/3.5oz=101m/110 yd): 1 ball each, colors (A) Happy Red #47 and (B) Jade #166—approx 201m/220yds of aran-weight yarn

- Knitting needles: 4mm (size 6 U.S.) 41cm/16" circular needle or size to obtain gauge
- 2 stitch markers
- Tapestry needle

GAUGE
- 15 sts/20 rnds = 10cm/4" worked on 4mm (size 6 U.S) needles in St st
- *Always take time to check your gauge.*

SPECIAL TECHNIQUES

The alternating wrap technique serves multiple purposes. It helps deal with long floats, gives the cowl a stiff body, and produces a tweedy effect by allowing the unused color to peek through from the back. The wrap has two parts.

- **Wrap Front** Wrap the unused color clockwise one time around the strand about to be knitted. Pull the unused color to the right side with your RH, knit the stitch as normal.

- **Wrap Back** Wrap the unused color counter clockwise one time around the strand about to be knitted. Pull the unused color to the right side with your RH, knit the stitch as normal.

Alternate these two wraps with each stitch whenever you're working two or more consecutive stitches in the same color. Alternating wraps in this way prevents the yarn from tangling.

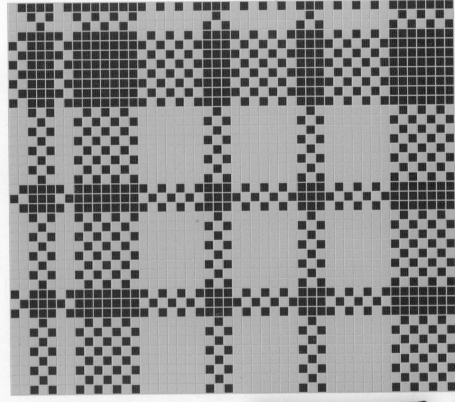

Instructions

With circular needle and A, cast on 96 sts. Join, being careful not to twist sts.

Using A, work 7 rnds in k2, p2 rib.

Next Rnd Using A, PM, k48, PM, k 48.

Next Rnd Join B. Incorporating alternating wraps, work 2 reps of chart across rnd (1 bet each marker). Cont to work to top of chart. End off B.

Next Rnd Using A, knit.

Using A, work 7 rnds in k2, p2 rib.

Cast off.

Finish

Weave in yarn ends.

The row of twinkling crystals
nestled in the folds of this cowl
is sure to catch attention. Pulling
the thread used to sew them on
gathers the cowl.

whisper

design by **AMY MICALLEF**

SKILL LEVEL
Intermediate

FINISHED MEASUREMENTS
23cm/9" in height; 71cm/28"
circumference

MATERIALS + TOOLS
- Rowan Kidsilk Haze (70% super kid mohair, 30% silk; 25g/85oz= 210m/229yds): 1 skein, color Heavenly #592—approx 210m/229yds of double knitting-weight yarn
- Knitting needles: 3.5mm (size 4 U.S.) 12"/31cm circular needle or size to obtain gauge
- Stitch marker
- Sewing needle
- Tapestry needle
- 4mm bicone crystals
  The number of crystals to use depends on how much bling and scrunch you desire. The cowl shown has 10 crystals, but you may use more than that.

GAUGE
- 22 sts/36 rows = 10 cm/4" worked on 3.5mm (size 4 U.S.) circular needle in St st.
- *Always take time to check your gauge.*

Instructions
Cast on 250 sts; join, being careful not to twist sts. Place marker at beg of rnd. Work 2 rnds in St st (knit every rnd).

Rnds 1, 3, and 5 Knit, dec 1 st every 10th st.

Rnd 2 and all even rnds Knit.

Rnd 7 Knit, dec 1 st every 9th st.

Rnd 9 Knit, dec 1 st every 8th st.

Rnd 11 Knit, dec 1 st every 7th st.

Rnd 13 Knit, dec 1 st every 6th st.

Rnd 15 Knit, dec 1 st every 5th st.

Rnd 17 Knit, dec 1 st every 4th st. Continue even in St st until piece measures 23cm/9", or desired length. Cast off, leaving a 31cm/12" tail.

Finish
Thread the tail into the needle and work running sts 6mm/¼" long straight across to the other edge of the tube. Flip the piece over and as you stitch again, following the stitching path back to its starting point, place beads on each RS fold. Pull the rest of the tail to cause the piece to scrunch, tightening it to the desired length. Tie off.

Weave in yarn ends.

Bright color punctuated by enormous pom-poms keeps it modern and gets you noticed.

crush

design by **TARA-LYNN MORRISON**

SKILL LEVEL
Easy

FINISHED MEASUREMENTS
20 x 53cm/8 x 21"

MATERIALS + TOOLS
- Any blended lamb's wool yarn, color orange—approx 137–183m/150–200yds chunky-weight yarn
- Knitting needles: 9mm (size 13 U.S.) 74cm/29" circular needle or size needed to obtain gauge
- Tapestry needle
- Scrap cardboard
- Sharp scissors

GAUGE
- 12 sts/20 rnds = 10cm/4" worked on 9mm (size 13 U.S.) circular needle in Moss St Pattern
- *Always take time to check your gauge.*

Instructions

Using circular needle, cast on 63 sets. Join, being careful not to twist sts.

Moss St Pattern

Rnd 1 K1, *p1, k1; rep from * around.
Rnd 2 P1, *k1, p1; rep from * around.
Rep Rnds 1 and 2 for Moss St patt + with a k st always over a p st and a p st always over a k st. Work until piece measures 20cm 8".

Cast off in Moss St.

Finish

Weave in yarn ends.

Drawstring

Cut a piece of yarn 127cm/50" long. Thread the tapestry needle and weave in and out of cowl every 5cm/2", approx 5cm/2" down from the top.

Pompoms
Make 2 extra-large pompoms:

Photocopy and cut out the C-shaped

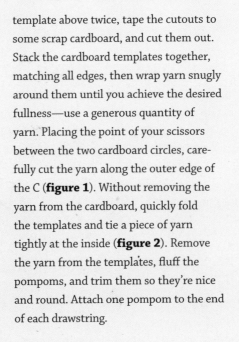

pompom template

template above twice, tape the cutouts to some scrap cardboard, and cut them out. Stack the cardboard templates together, matching all edges, then wrap yarn snugly around them until you achieve the desired fullness—use a generous quantity of yarn. Placing the point of your scissors between the two cardboard circles, carefully cut the yarn along the outer edge of the C (**figure 1**). Without removing the yarn from the cardboard, quickly fold the templates and tie a piece of yarn tightly at the inside (**figure 2**). Remove the yarn from the templates, fluff the pompoms, and trim them so they're nice and round. Attach one pompom to the end of each drawstring.

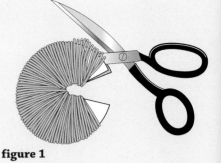

figure 1

figure 2

58

An unusual cable structure gives this cowl lots of visually interesting folds and textures.

dreamy

design by **JANNA MARIA VALLÉE**

SKILL LEVEL
Easy

FINISHED MEASUREMENTS
20cm/8" wide; 64cm/25" upper circumference; 94cm/37" bottom circumference

MATERIALS + TOOLS
- Colossal Cozy hand-spun, hand-dyed yarn in Tropical Sea by Janna Maria (or substitute any chunky-weight yarn that matches gauge), 150g/5oz= 90m/98yds, 1 skein, color turquoise— approx 190m/98yds of extra chunky-weight yarn
- Knitting needles: 10mm (size 15 U.S.) circular needle, 80cm/32" long or size needed to obtain gauge
- One large cable needle
- Tapestry needle

GAUGE
- 7 sts/12 rnds = 10cm/4" worked on 10mm (size 15 U.S.) circular needle in St st
- *Always take time to check your gauge.*

Instructions
Cast on 50 sts. Join, being careful not to twist sts.

Rnd 1 P15, k20, p15.

Rnds 2–12 Rep Rnd 1.

Rnd 13 P15, sl 10 sts onto cn and hold at back of work, k10, k10 from cn, p15.

Rnds 14–18 P15, k20, p15.

Rnd 19 P13, p2tog, k20, p2tog, p13—48 sts.

Rnd 20 P12, p2tog, k20, p2tog, p12—46 sts.

Rnd 21 P11, p2tog, k20, p2tog, p11—44 sts.

Rnd 22 P10, p2tog, k20, p2tog, p10—42 sts.

Rnd 23 P9, p2tog, k20, p2tog, p9—40 sts.

Rnd 24 Cast off.

Finish
Weave in any loose ends.

Think those are pom-
poms? Look closer:
those little puffballs
are actually knitted
and stuffed.

sugar

design by **LANA O'NEILL**

SKILL LEVEL
Easy

FINISHED MEASUREMENT
25 x 58cm/10 x 23" in circumference

MATERIALS + TOOLS
- Cascade 220 (100% wool; 100g/3.5oz=
  201m/220yds); 2 skeins, color White
  #8505—approx 402m/440yds aran-
  weight yarn

- Knitting needles: 3.75mm (size 5 U.S.)
  circular needle, 41cm/16" long; 3.5mm
  (size 4 U.S.) double-pointed needles or
  size to obtain gauge
- Stitch markers
- Fiberfill
- Tapestry needle

GAUGE
- 16 sts = 10cm/4" worked on 3.75mm
  (size 5 U.S.) circular needle in rib
- *Always take time to check your gauge.*

Instructions

Cowl

Using circular needle, cast on 92 sts. Mark the last st with a st marker, then join and work in rnds as foll: Work around in k2, p2 rib until piece measures 8cm/3" from beg.

Next Rnd *K1, k2tog twice, k1, (p2, k2) for next 18 sts; rep from * 2 more times, k1, k2tog twice, k1, (p2, k2) rib to end of rnd—84 sts.

Next Rnd *K2tog twice, work in est rib on next 18 sts; rep from * 2 more times, k2tog twice, (p2, k2) rib to end of rnd—76 sts.

Cont around in k2, p2 rib until cowl measures 26cm/10" from beg.

Eyelet patt *K2, yo, p2tog; rep from * around.

Cont in k2, p2 rib for 3 more rnds. Cast off.

I-Cord

Using dpn, cast on 3 sts. *K3 sts. Do not turn the work. Slide sts to right end of the needle, pull yarn to tighten; rep from * until the cord measures 140cm/55". Cast off and thread the cord through the eyelets of the turtleneck cowl.

Balls

Pick up 6 sts at the end of the cord.

Inc Rnd *K1 st, pick up 1 st by inserting a needle into the loop of the st 1 rnd below and k through it, rep from * until you have 12 sts.

Divide 12 sts evenly on 3 dpns. Join and knit around for 9 rnds.

Insert fiberfill stuffing inside the knitted ball piece.

Dec Rnd *K2tog; rep from * around—6 sts rem.

Cut off the yarn, leaving enough to sew rem sts together. Thread the yarn through the tapestry needle and draw the yarn through the rem sts. Fasten off.

Rep the same process at the other end of the cord.

To make 2 extra balls, pick up 3 sts from the I-cord, approximately 8–10cm/3–4" from the edge. Work the I-cord approximately 8–10cm/3–4" or to the desired length, then pick up 6 sts at the end of the cord and work the ball as above.

Rep the same process at the other end of the cord.

Finish

Weave in yarn ends.

VARIATIONS

Make the I-cord different lengths so the balls are at different heights; when the ties are tied at the neck, they'll appear to cascade down. You can also stick to making only 2 balls, instead of 4.

A lightweight cowl tossed casually over the shoulders conveys your light-hearted attitude.

frivolous

design by **JOLYNN BURT**

SKILL LEVEL
Intermediate

FINISHED MEASUREMENTS
36cm/14" wide; 66cm/26" circumference

MATERIALS + TOOLS
- NaturallyCaron.com Spa (25% bamboo, 75% microdenier acrylic; 85g/3oz= 230m/251yds): 2 skeins, color Berry Frappe #006—approx 459m/502yds of aran-weight yarn

- Knitting needles: 4.5mm and 5.5mm (sizes 7 and 9 U.S.) circular needles or size to obtain gauge
- Stitch marker
- Tapestry needle

GAUGE
- 20 sts = 10cm/4" worked on 4.5mm (size 7 U.S.) needles in pattern
- *Always take time to check your gauge.*

STITCH PATTERN

Rnd 1 K5, *p5, k5; rep from * around, end p5.

Rnd 2 *K5, p5; rep from * around.

Rnd 3 P1, *k5, p5; rep from * around, end k5, p4.

Rnd 4 P2, *k5, p5; rep from * around, end k5, p3.

Rnd 5 P3, *k5, p5; rep from * around, end k5, p2.

Rnd 6 P4, *k5, p5; rep from * around, end k5, p1.

Rnd 7 P5, *k5, p5; * rep from * around, end k5.

Rnd 8 K1, *p5, k5; rep from * around, end p5, k4.

Rnd 9 K2, *p5, k5; rep from * around, end p5, k3.

Rnd 10 K3, *p5, k5; rep from * around, end p5, k2.

Rnd 11 K4, *p5, k5; rep from * around, end p5, k1.

Rep Rnds 2–11 for patt.

KNIT CAST-ON METHOD

Leave a 26cm/10" tail (to sew the seam later) and make a slip knot. Place the slip knot on the knitting needle. Knit into this st but don't remove it from the left needle. Place the right needle loop back onto the left needle and rep until desired number of sts are cast on.

Instructions

With 4.5mm (size 7 U.S.) needle, cast on 260 sts using Knit cast-on method (described below left) Do not join; work back and forth on circular needle.

Knit 7 rows.

Next Row *K2tog; rep from * across— 130 sts.

Join, being careful not to twist sts. Place a marker at beg of rnd.

Work around in pattern for 28cm/11".

Next Rnd Knit into front and back of each st—260 sts. Turn and work back and forth on circular needle.

Knit 7 rows.

With 5.5mm (size 9 U.S.) needle, cast on. Leave a 26cm/10" tail. Sew the ruffle carefully.

Finish

Weave in yarn ends.

There's no way you can go wrong with a huge cowl knitted from chunky yarn. Make it in the most eye-catching color you can find.

catch

design by **MARY JANE BARRY**

SKILL LEVEL
Easy

FINISHED MEASUREMENTS
51 x 86 cm/20 x 34" in circumference

MATERIALS + TOOLS
- Lion Brand Wool-Ease Thick & Quick (80% wool, 20% acrylic; 142g/5oz= 97m/106yds): 2 skeins, color Lemongrass #640-132—approx 194m/212yds of extra chunky-weight yarn
- Knitting needles 12mm (size 17 U.S.) circular needles, 74cm/29"/long
- Tapestry needle

GAUGE
- 8 sts/10 rnds = 10cm/4" worked on 12mm (size 17 U.S.) needles in St st
- *Always take time to check your gauge.*

Instructions
Cast on 61 sts. Allow needle to twist once (to create Möbius strip), join ends, and thread end of cast-on yarn through first cast-on st to secure ends.

Rnd 1 Knit.

Rnds 2–60 Cont to knit until Rnd 60 or until all yarn is finished, leaving enough to cast off.

Cast off all sts on last rnd.

Finish
Weave in yarn ends.

Wear it loose around the neck, wear it up over your head, but wear it often. Make it in a pretty color that makes your skin glow.

design by **ROSARIO THURY CORNEJO**

glances

SKILL LEVEL
Easy

FINISHED MEASUREMENTS
- 24 x 66cm/9½ x 26" before sewing

MATERIALS + TOOLS
- Lion Brand Wool-Ease Thick & Quick (80% wool, 20% acrylic; 170g/6oz= 97m/106yds): 1 skein, color #640-112 Raspberry—approx 97m/106yds of extra chunky-weight yarn
- Knitting needles: 9mm (size 13 U.S.) or size needed to obtain gauge
- Small amount of waste yarn in contrasting color
- Tapestry needle

GAUGE
- 9 sts/16 rows = 10cm/4" worked on 9mm (size 13 U.S) needles in Garter st
- *Always take time to check your gauge.*

Instructions

Cast on 24 sts using the waste yarn.

Change to main color yarn, leaving a short tail. Work in Garter st (k every row) for 112 rows.

Lay out and fold as shown in the illustration, then bring C and D onto A and B, respectively **(figure 1)**. The result should look like **figure 2**.

Work grafting st as follows: Remove the waste yarn on the top part and replace the loops on a needle. Insert the threaded tapestry needle into the first st at the RH edge of the upper piece. Put the needle down through the 1st st on the lower piece and bring it up through the next st. Bring the needle up through the 1st st on the upper piece and put it down through the next st. The needle's path is up-down on the upper piece, down-up on the lower piece, inserting the needle knitwise with up meaning purlwise; you p the upper row of sts and k the lower row **(figure 3)**. Rep until all the sts are joined.

Finish

Weave in yarn ends.

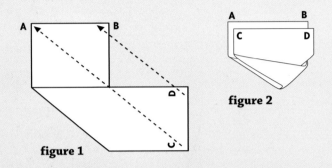

figure 1

figure 2

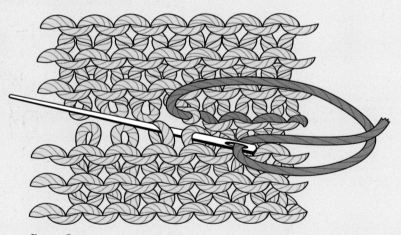

figure 3

Go on, gush to your best friend about how wonderful your sweetie is. She'll be happy for you, but she'll also be wishing she owned your cool ruched cowl.

wish

design by **CARRIE APPLE EDDLEMAN**

SKILL LEVEL
Easy

FINISHED MEASUREMENTS
- 30cm/12" in height; 76cm/30" circumference

MATERIALS + TOOLS
- Lion Brand Vanna's Choice (100% acrylic; 100g/3.5oz= 156m/170yds): 2 skeins, color Eggplant #860-145— approx 312m/340yds of aran-weight yarn
- Knitting needles: 6mm (size 10 U.S.) or size to obtain gauge
- Tapestry needle

GAUGE
- 14 sts = 10cm/4" worked on 6mm (size 10 U.S.) needles in pattern st
- *Always take time to check your gauge.*

Instructions
Cast on 40 sts.

Rows 1–6 Knit.

Row 7 (RS) Inc 1 st in each st—80 sts.

Row 8 Purl.

Row 9 Knit.

Row 10 Purl.

Row 11 Knit.

Row 12 Purl.

Row 13 (RS) *K2tog; rep from * across.

Rep Rows 1–13 until piece measures approx 76cm/30", ending with Row 13: k2tog, *k2tog, cast off, rep from * across.

Finish
Sew ends together to create a cowl.

Weave in yarn ends.

flirt rapt giddy breathless tickle blush dizzy

collars

COLLARS, those dapper little accessories—think of them as trims and garnishes that fit snugly at the neck. Most of the projects in this section fasten on with buttons, but you've probably caught on by now that a few outliers, too cool to leave out on technicalities, got included.

Now, on a blouse, it's probably a good idea to limit collar length and keep the look kind of crisp and prim, but there's no reason to be so buttoned down when it comes to knitwear. While there are some relatively restrained designs in this section, you also have the option of more length, as shown in the project on the next page, and can even blow it out with a dazzling corkscrew coil that falls almost to the belly button (page 98). As in previous sections of this book, you'll find a focus on texture and pattern.

Meeting that
special someone for
drinks after work?
Get pretty in a wide
cabled collar.

flirt

design by **BRENDA LAVELL**

SKILL LEVEL
Intermediate

FINISHED MEASUREMENTS
21cm x 86cm/8¼ x 34"

MATERIALS + TOOLS
- Lion Brand Wool-Ease Thick & Quick (80% wool, 20% acrylic; 170g/6oz= 97m/106yds): 2 skeins, color Citron #640-134—approx 194m/212yds of extra chunky-weight yarn
- Knitting needles: 12mm (size 17 U.S.) or size to obtain gauge
- 1 large cable or double-pointed needle
- 1 button, 4cm/1½" in diameter
- 2 buttons, 2.5cm/1" in diameter
- Thread in color matching yarn
- 2 small pieces of wool or felt to stabilize the button (optional)
- Sewing needle
- Tapestry needle

GAUGE
- 8 sts/12 rows = 10cm/4" worked on 12mm (size 17 U.S.) needles in St st, after blocking
- Cable Panel = 15cm/6" worked on 12mm (size 17 U.S) needles in St st, after blocking, measured from the widest part of the large cable edge
- *Always take time to check your gauge.*

SPECIAL ABBREVIATIONS
- **ICR (RS I-cord edge)** First 3 and last 3 sts of every RS row: K1, sl 1 pwise wyif, k1.
- **ICW (WS I-cord edge)** First 3 and last 3 sts of every WS row: Sl 1 pwise wyif, k1, sl 1 pwise wyif.

NOTE
For longer length, add one Body repeat for each 15cm/6" of desired length (additional ⅓ skein or 52m/57yds of yarn for each additional 15cm/6").

Instructions

Front/Top Flap

Cast on 30 sts.

Row 1 (RS) ICR, p2, k3, p4, k6, p4, k3, p2, ICR.

Row 2 and all even numbered rows (WS) ICW, k the k sts and p the p sts to within last 3 sts, ICW.

Rows 3–6 Rep Rows 1–2 twice.

Row 7 ICR, p2, (sl 3 to cn or dpn and hold in front, p2, k3 from cn), p2, k6, p2, (sl 2 to cn and hold in back, k3, p2 from cn), p2, ICR.

Row 9 ICR, p4, (sl 3 to cn and hold in front, p2, k3 from cn), (sl 3 to cn and hold in front, k3, k3 from cn), (sl 2 to cn and hold in back, k3, p2 from cn), p4, ICR.

Row 11 ICR, p6, *(sl 3 to cn and hold in back, k3, k3 from cn)*, rep from * to *, p6, ICR.

Row 13 ICR, p6, k3, (sl 3 to cn and hold in front, k3, k3 from cn), k3, p6, ICR.

Row 15 ICR, p4, (sl 2 to cn and hold in back, k3, p2 from cn), k6, (sl 3 to cn and hold in front, p2, k3 from cn), p4, ICR.

Row 17 ICR, p2, (sl 2 to cn and hold in back, k3, p2 from cn), p2, k6, p2, (sl 3 to cn and hold in front, p2, k3 from cn), p2, ICR.

Row 18 Rep Row 2.

Body

Row 19 Rep Row 1.

Row 21 Rep Row 7.

Row 23 Rep Row 9.

Row 25 Rep Row 11.

Row 27 Rep Row 13.

Row 29 ICR, p6, *(sl 3 to cn and hold in back, k3, k3 from cn)*, rep from * to *, p6, ICR.

Row 31 ICR, p4, (sl 2 to cn and hold in back, k3, p2 from cn), (sl 3 to cn and hold in front, p3, k3 from cn), (sl 3 to hold in front, k3, p2 from cn), p4, ICR.

Row 33 Rep Row 17.

Row 34 Rep Row 18.

Rep Rows 19–34 three more times (4 total cable patt reps).

Bottom Flap

Rep Rows 1–2 for 12 total rows, ending WS.

Purl, cast off in patt.

Weave in ends (utilize the I-cord edge and cables to hide and secure ends).

Finish

Block to measurements. Weave in yarn ends.

Note Before attaching the buttons, read these directions carefully and check your own finished cowl to mark the best attachment spots.

Securely attach the large button to the center end of the bottom flap. First attach the felt pieces to the flap, bottom and top, then sew the button through all 3 layers (felt, knitted cowl, felt) to provide stability and strength during buttoning. The button will slip through the small opening in the very first cable cross on the top flap.

Attach each smaller button underneath the top flap, approximately 2 I-cord sts from the end and one I-cord st from the side, securely sewing through the I-cord sts while avoiding showing the stitching through the front of the flap. The buttons will slip through a st (no buttonhole needed) on the under flap.

A knitted collar edged with crocheted eyelash yarn brings the attention up to your gorgeous face. In a multicolored yarn, it can match nearly any outfit.

tickle

design by **IRINA GRINEVITSKY**

SKILL LEVEL
Easy

FINISHED MEASUREMENTS
9 x 51cm/3½ x 20"

MATERIALS + TOOLS
- Lion Brand Chenille Thick & Quick (91% acrylic, 9% rayon; 100g/3.5oz= 68m/75yds): (A) 1 ball, color Desert Print—approx 68m/75yds of extra chunky-weight yarn
- Lion Brand Fun Fur Exotics (100% polyester; 50g/1.75oz= 50m/55yds): (B) 1 ball, color Oxyx #320-150—approximately 50m/55yds of sport-weight yarn
- Knitting needles: 9mm (size 13 U.S.) or size needed to obtain gauge
- 5mm (size H-8 U.S.) crochet hook
- 1 round pearl button, 2.5cm/1" in diameter
- Tapestry needle

GAUGE
- 8 sts/10 rows = 10cm/4" worked on 9mm (size 13 U.S.) needle in rib
- *Always take time to check your gauge.*

Instructions
With A, cast on 8 sts.
Work in k1, p1 rib for approx 50 rows or 51cm/20".
  Cast off.

Finish
With RS facing, using crochet hook and B, work 1 sc in every other row around entire scarf to make a border of eyelash yarn. Weave in yarn ends.

Sew the button approx 2.5cm/1" from one end. Sts are loose enough that a buttonhole isn't necessary.

Not getting your way? This texture-laden collar will make you feel so snug and happy you won't be able to mope for long.

pout

design by **SIMONE MEYER**

SKILL LEVEL
Easy

FINISHED MEASUREMENTS
23 x 91cm/9 x 36" at widest points

MATERIALS + TOOLS
- Classic Elite Twinkle Soft Chunky (100% wool; 200g/7oz = 76m/83yd): 1 skein, color Spruce #36—approx 79m/83yd of extra chunky-weight yarn
- Knitting needles: 12mm (size 17 U.S.) 41cm/16" circular or straight needles or size to obtain gauge
- 2 toggle buttons, 5cm/2" in diameter
- Tapestry needle

GAUGE
- 7 sts/29 rows = 10cm/4" worked on 12mm (size 17 U.S.) needles in Moss Stitch
- *Always take time to check your gauge.*

SPECIAL ABBREVIATIONS
- **M1** Make one st by picking up the loop between the st just worked and the next st, and knit into the loop.
- **Ssk** Slip the next st as if to knit, slip another st as if to knit, insert point of left needle into the two slipped sts in front of the right needle and knit the two slipped sts together.

NOTE
Collar is worked in Seed Stitch with a knit st always over a purl st and a purl st always over a knit st.

Instructions

Cast on 4 sts.

Row 1 (WS) K1, p1, k1, p1.

Row 2 (RS) K1, M1, k1, p1, M1, k1.

Row 3 *P1, k1; rep from * to end.

Row 4 K1, M1, *p1, k1; rep from * to last st, M1, k1.

Row 5 *K1, p1; rep from * to end.

Row 6 K1, M1, *k1, p1; rep from * to last st, M1, k1.

Row 7 *P1, k1; rep from * to end.

Row 8 *K1, p1; rep from * to end.

Row 9 *P1, k1; rep from * to end.

Rows 10–17 Rep last 2 rows.

Row 18 K1, M1, *p1, k1; rep from * to last st, M1, k1—12 sts.

Row 19 *K1, p1; rep from * to end.

Row 20 *P1, k1; rep from * to end.

Rows 21–33 Rep last 2 rows.

Row 34 K1, M1, *k1, p1; rep from * to last st, M1, k1—14 sts.

Row 35 *P1, k1; rep from * to end.

Row 36 *K1, p1; rep from * to end.

Rows 37–43 Rep last 2 rows.

Row 44 K1, M1, *p1, k1; rep from * to last st, M1, k1—16 sts.

Row 45 *K1, p1; rep from * to end.

Row 46 *P1, k1; rep from * to end.

Rows 47–70 Rep last 2 rows.

Row 71 Ssk, *k1, p1; rep from * to last 2 sts, k2tog—14 sts.

Row 72 *K1, p1; rep from * to end.

Row 73 *P1, k1; rep from * to end.

Rows 74–86 Rep last 2 rows.

Row 87 Ssk, *p1, k1; rep from * to last 2 sts, k2tog—12 sts.

Row 88 *P1, k1; rep from * to end.

Row 89 *K1, p1; rep from * to end.

Rows 90–98 Rep last 2 rows.

Row 99 Ssk, *k1, p1; rep from * to last 2 sts, k2tog—10 sts.

Row 100 *K1, p1; rep from * to end.

Row 101 Ssk, *p1, k1; rep from * to last 2 sts, k2tog—8 sts.

Row 102 *P1, k1; rep from * to end.

Row 103 Ssk, *k1, p1; rep from * to last 2 sts, k2tog—6 sts.

Row 104 *K1, p1; rep from * to end.

Row 105 Ssk, p1, k1, k2tog—4 sts.

Cast off.

Finish

Weave in yarn ends. Attach both buttons to the RS of the collar, the first one 8.9cm/3½" from one end, the other 29cm/11½" from the same end, and both centered along the accessory.

Elegant but softly shaped, this collar has crossed ends that echo the intersecting cables in its motif.

design by **LINDA LUNN**

breathless

SKILL LEVEL
Intermediate

FINISHED MEASUREMENTS
25 x 76cm/10 x 30"

MATERIALS + TOOLS
- Rowan Big Wool (100% merino wool; 99g/3.5oz= 80m/87yds): 2 balls, color Latte #018—approx 159m/174yds of extra chunky-weight yarn
- Knitting needles: 10mm (size 15 U.S.) or size needed to obtain gauge
- Row counter
- 2 large wooden buttons, 5cm x 4cm/ 2 x 1½"
- Tapestry needle

GAUGE
- 7½ sts and 9 rows = 10cm/4" worked on 10mm (size 15 U.S.) in St st
- *Always take time to check your gauge.*

Instructions

Cast on 22 sts.

Use a row counter to keep count of all rows. Purl 3 rows.

**Next Row (RS) K6, k2tog, k2, yf, k5, yf, k2, k2tog, k3.

Row (WS) K2, purl to last 2 sts, k2.

Next Row K5, k2tog, k2, yf, k1, yf, k2, k2tog, k8.

Next Row K2, p to last 2 sts, k2.

Next Row K4, k2tog, k2, yf, k3, yf, k2, k2tog, k7.

Next Row K2, p to last 2 sts, k2.*

Next Row K3, k2tog, k2, yf, k5, yf, k2, k2tog, k6.

Next Row K2, p to last 2 sts, k2.

Next Row K8, k2tog, k2, yf, k1, yf, k2, k2tog, k5.

Next Row K2, p to last 2 sts, k2.

Next Row K7, k2tog, k2, yf, k3, yf, k2, k2tog, k4.

Next Row K2, p to last 2 sts, k2.**

Rep from ** to ** 5 more times.

Rep from ** to * once. There should be 81 rows completed from cast off.

Purl 2 rows.

Cast off all sts pwise.

Finish

Weave in ends. Soak in cool water for 20 minutes. Roll in towel to squeeze out the excess water, and lay flat to dry.

Sew buttons at desired position. Eyelets in the pattern will serve as buttonholes.

Wait for a friend in style while wearing a remarkable collar. It closes with a toggle, leaving an appealing bit of skin showing.

design by **EWELINA OLESINSKA**

giddy

SKILL LEVEL
Easy

FINISHED MEASUREMENTS
20 x 46cm/8 x 18"

MATERIALS + TOOLS
- Patons Decor (25% wool, 75% acrylic; 100g/3.5oz= 190m/208yds): 1 skein, color (A) Burnt Orange #87605, 1 skein color (B) Chocolate Taupe #87633— approx 215m/236yds of aran-weight yarn
- Knitting needles: 4.5mm (size 7 U.S.) or size to obtain gauge
- Cable needle
- Toggle, 4cm/1½", in dark brown leather
- Sewing needle
- Dark brown thread
- Tapestry needle

GAUGE
- 20 sts/26 rows = 10cm/4" worked on 4.5mm (size 7 U.S.) needles in St st
- *Always take time to check your gauge.*

Instructions

With B, cast on 122 sts (120 for patt plus 2 for edges).

Rows 1–3 Beg on WS with a purl row, work in St st for 3 rows. Change to A.

Row 4 Foll diagram beg with Row 1 as foll: The 1st and last st as edge sts (marked x on the diagram) are not included in the patt. The edge chain st is achieved by knitting the 1st st and slipping the last st of each row.

Only odd rows are marked on the diagram. In all even-numbered rows, every previously k st should be now worked as a p st.

Work the 24-st pat rep 5 times in each row and finish with the edge st (rep part is marked on the diagram). This makes the circumference of the collar.

Work the 14-row rep 3 times and rep the pat as shown on the diagram. After finishing the last 14th row, work the next 2 rows the same way as the 1st 2 rows of the patt (k 1 row and p 1 row).

Work the last 3 rows with B in St st, same as the 1st 3 rows.

Cast off all sts.

Finish

Weave in yarn ends. Sew on the toggle to both edges at the desired distance apart.

■ CABLE BAND

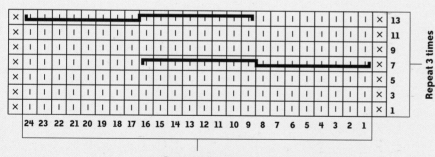

Repeat 3 times

24 23 22 21 20 19 18 17 16 15 14 13 12 11 10 9 8 7 6 5 4 3 2 1

Repeat 5 times

■ CHART KEY

 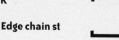

| × | K |
| ı | Edge chain st |

 Place 8 sts on a cable needle, hold in front of work, then k8 from cable needle

Place 8 sts on a cable needle, hold in back of work, then k8 from cable needle

It's all about scale: a chunky collar ties closed with crosses made of wide grosgain ribbon in a complementary color.

blush

design by **JOANNA BOXALL**

SKILL LEVEL
Easy

FINISHED MEASUREMENTS
15 x 53cm/6 x 21"

MATERIALS + TOOLS
- Twilleys of Stamford Freedom Wool (100% wool; 50g/1.75oz= 50m/55yds): 2 skeins, color Deep Red—approx 100m/109yds of extra chunky-weight yarn
- Knitting needles: 10mm (size 15 U.S.) or size to obtain gauge
- 2.25m/2½ yds of 2.5cm/1" wide navy satin ribbon
- Tapestry needle

GAUGE
- 8 sts/14 rows = 10cm/4" worked on 10mm (size 15 U.S.) needles in Garter st
- *Always take time to check your gauge.*

Instructions
Cast on 24 sts.
    Work in Garter st (knit every row) for 74 rows.
    Cast off knitwise.

Finish
Neatly weave in all loose threads along edges. Fold knitted piece in half lengthwise.

At cast-on and cast-off edges, thread ribbon through the double layer of knitting creating a laced-up effect and joining two ends of knitting tog.

At the bottom of the laced-up knitting, tie the ribbon in a bow and trim the edges of ribbon to your preferred length.

dizzy

design by **LEIGH-ANNE FREDERICK**

Ruffles, ruffles, ruffles. As light glints off the metallic yarn in this collar, it puts you in the spotlight. Shine on, you crazy diamond!

SKILL LEVEL
Easy

FINISHED MEASUREMENTS
41cm/16" at neck; 26 x 69cm/10 x 27" at collar edge

MATERIALS + TOOLS
■ Lion Brand Moonlight Mohair (57% acrylic, 28% mohair, 9% cotton, 6% metallic polyester; 50g/1.75oz= 75m/82yds): 2 balls, color Tundra #510202—approx 150m/164yds of chunky-weight yarn

■ Knitting needles: 5mm and 6.5mm (sizes 8 and 10-½ U.S.) or size needed to obtain gauge
■ Stitch marker
■ 2 vintage buttons, 15–18mm/½–¾" in diameter
■ Tapestry needle

GAUGE
■ 12 sts/18 rows = 10cm/4" worked on 6.5mm (size 10-½ U.S.) needles in St st.
■ *Always take time to check your gauge.*

NOTE
For a lacier look, use a larger needle size.

CHOOSING YARN

This pattern can be completed in any yarn. Just work to the gauge given on the packaging. Using the stitches and rows per cm/inch, you can calculate the appropriate number of stitches to cast on. Simply multiply the sts per cm/inch x 5 (or the desired width). Adjust the short row pattern to accommodate the number of stitches being used. Continue in this pattern until you obtain the desired length. When knitting the Neck Band portion, use a needle size that is 1.5 sizes smaller than the one used for the Jabot and Ruff.

Instructions

Jabot

Using size 6.5mm (size 10½ U.S.) needles, cast on 15 sts.
Work 2 rows in St st.
Buttonhole Row K12 sts, (yo, k2tog) for buttonhole, k1.
Purl 1 row.
Work 2 more rows in St st.

Beg short rows as follows:
**Next Row (RS) K12 sts, turn.
Next Row and every WS row Purl.
Next RS Row K10 sts, turn.
Next RS Row K8 sts, turn.
Next RS Row K6 sts, turn.
Next RS Row K4 sts, turn.
Next RS row K2 sts, turn.
Knit 2 rows in St st across all sts.**
Rep from ** to ** until piece, when measured on the short side, measures approx 68.5cm/27" long.
Note If working to the correct tension, this should be a total of 35 short row pattern reps. At this point the length can be altered by either increasing or decreasing the number of reps completed. Be sure to always end at ** of the pattern sequence.
Cast off loosely.

Neck Band

Using 5mm (size 8 U.S.) needles and WS facing (purl side), and starting on RH side (buttonhole edge), measure 43cm/17" across the short edge of the piece and place a marker. Pick up and knit approx 4 sts for every 5 rows of knitting to the marker (approx 49–51 sts).

Note To change the size, the collar length can be adjusted by picking up more or less sts, making sure to have an uneven number.
WS has now become the RS.
Next Row With WS facing (knit side), (p1, k1) to end of row.
Next Row (RS) (K1, p1) to end of row.
Rep these 2 rows for a total of 7 rows of rib.
Next Row (RS) K1, p1, (yo, k2tog) for second buttonhole, continue in rib to the end of row.
Work 3 more rows in rib.

Ruff

Change to 6.5mm (size 10½ U.S.) needles.
Work 8 rows in St st.
Cast off loosely.

Finish

Sew on buttons. Weave in yarn ends.

basic
techniques

slipknot longtail purl garter knit slip stitch   cast off yarn over make1

SLIPKNOT

Slipknots are used in knitting and crochet to cast on the first stitch of a project. Start by leaving a tail, then make a loop with the yarn that looks like a cursive e **(figure 1)** . Holding the area where the yarn crosses with one hand, push a new loop through the existing loop with your other hand **(figure 2)**. Place the new loop on the needle or hook and tighten both yarn ends to create the slipknot **(figure 3)**.

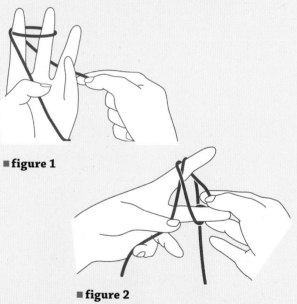

■ figure 1

■ figure 2

■ figure 3

LONGTAIL (DOUBLE) CAST-ON

Calculate about 2.5 cm (1 inch) of yarn per stitch that you'll be casting on; this will be your tail.

Letting the tail hang, tie a slipknot around one of your knitting needles. You'll now have two strands of yarn hanging down from your needle—the tail and the strand connected to the ball **(figure 4)**. Placing the needle in your right hand, separate the two strands of yarn with your left thumb and index finger. Secure both loose ends under your ring finger and little finger **(figure 5)**. *continues on next page*

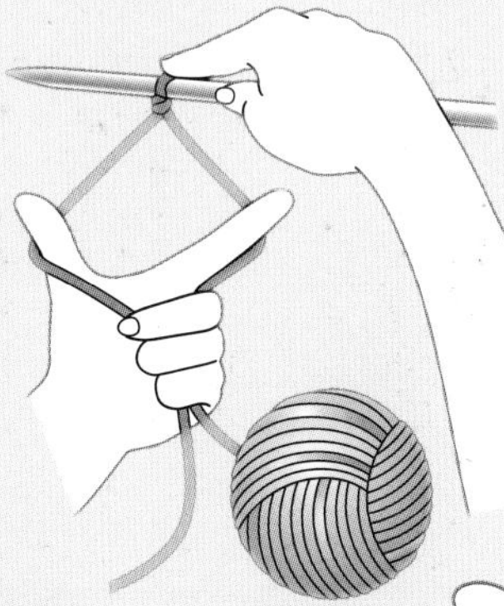

■ figure 4

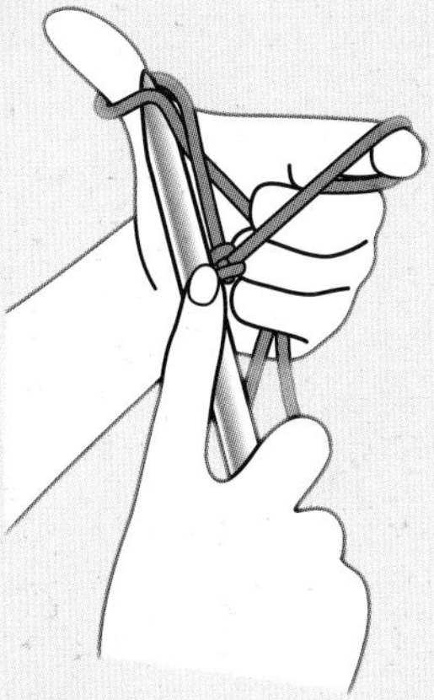

■ figure 5

LONGTAIL (DOUBLE) CAST-ON (continued)

Use your needle to scoop under the outer strand of the thumb loop **(figure 6)** then over the inner strand of the index finger loop **(figure 7)**. Let the loop fall off your thumb **(figure 8)** and pull the tail so that the stitch fits loosely onto your needle. Repeat until you've cast on the desired number of stitches.

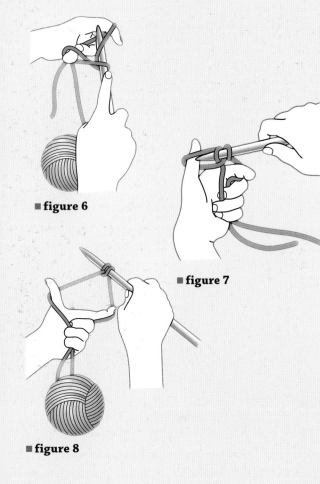

■ figure 6

■ figure 7

■ figure 8

KNIT STITCH

For the knit stitch, hold the needle with stitches on it in your left hand; the working yarn is held in your right hand and in the back of the work. Insert the right-hand needle, from bottom to top, into the stitch as shown in **figure 9**. The tips of the needles will form an x. Use your right index finger to wrap the strand of yarn, anticlockwise, around the right-hand needle **(figure 10)**.

Bring the yarn through the stitch with the right-hand needle and pull the loop off the left-hand needle **(figure 11)**. You now have one complete knit stitch on your right-hand needle.

Continue until the end of the row, or as the pattern directs.

■ figure 9

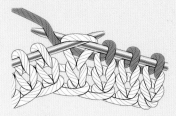

■ figure 10

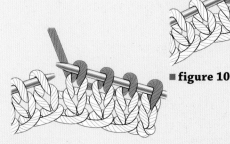

■ figure 11

PURL STITCH

For the purl stitch, hold the needle with the stitches on it in your left hand; the working yarn is held in the right hand and in front of your work. Insert the right-hand needle, from top to bottom, into the stitch **(figure 12)**. Using your right index finger, wrap the strand of yarn counterclockwise around the right-hand needle **(figure 13)**. Bring the yarn through the stitch with the right-hand needle and pull the loop off the left-hand needle **(figure 14)**. Continue until the end of the row, or as the pattern directs.

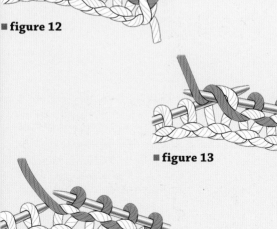

■ **figure 12**

■ **figure 13**

■ **figure 14**

STOCKING STITCH

This is probably what you think of when you hear "knitted." To do stocking, you alternate knit and purl rows, or, if you're working on circular needles, knit every row. Both sides of the stitch are shown here—what's generally considered the right side at top, with the wrong side (also called reverse stocking) beneath it. Reverse stocking is so pretty that it's frequently chosen to show on the exterior of a garment.

GARTER STITCH

This attractive stitch consists of nothing more than doing knit stitch every row.

PICKING UP STITCHES

To pick up stitches along a cast-off edge, insert your needle into the space under both loops of the existing stitch **(figure 15)**. Bring the yarn under the needle and scoop it through the hole to create one stitch on the needle. *Insert the needle into the next space, wrap the yarn counterclockwise, and scoop the loop through the space. Repeat from * until you've picked up the desired number of stitches **(figure 16)**.

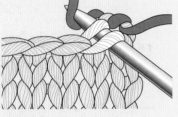

■ **figure 15**

■ **figure 16**

YARN OVER

Bring the working yarn to the front and knit the stitch normally. This wraps the yarn around the needle, creating a yarn over.

INC1 (MAKE 1 INCREASE)

With the right-hand needle, pick up the loop at the base of the next stitch on the left-hand needle. Place the loop on the left-hand needle. Treat the loop as a new stitch and knit into it normally.

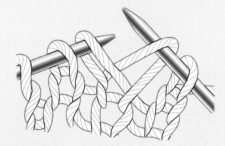

SLIP, SLIP, KNIT

Slip your next two stitches, one at a time, to the right-hand needle. Insert the tip of the left-hand needle into the fronts of these stitches, from left to right, and knit them together (= two stitches decreased).

SLIP STITCH PURLWISE

Slipping a stitch means you pass a stitch from one needle to another without working it. A slipstitch purlwise won't twist like it does knitwise. To slip one stitch purlwise, insert your right needle into the next stitch on your left needle as though purling the stitch. Pull the stitch off your left needle; the stitch will now be on the right needle.

CAST OFF

Knit two stitches. *With the tip of your left-hand needle, pull the second stitch on the right-hand needle over the first **(figure 17)** and let it drop off. You'll now have one stitch left on the needle **(figure 18)**. Knit another stitch and repeat from * **(figure 19)**.

Continue in this manner, or as the pattern directs.

SEWN CAST-OFF

Break off a length of yarn about three times as long as the knitting, and thread it onto a yarn needle. *Insert the needle into the first 2 stitches on the knitting needle as if to purl and draw the yarn through **(figure 20)**. Reinsert the needle into the first stitch on the knitting needle as if to knit, draw yarn though, then slip the stitch off. **(figure 21)*** Repeat from * to *.

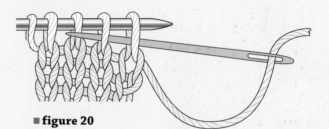

■ **figure 20**

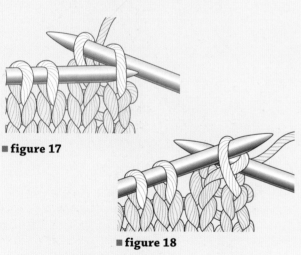

■ **figure 17**

■ **figure 18**

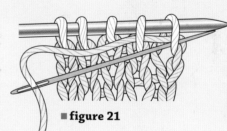

■ **figure 21**

■ **figure 19**

WEAVE IN ENDS

Using a tapestry needle, weave the loose ends of yarn in and out of the stitches on the wrong side of the work. Whenever possible, weave the ends into seam lines.

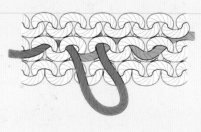

DOUBLE CROCHET

Insert the hook into both loops of the stitch from the row below, as shown in **figure 22**. Wrap the yarn anticlockwise around the hook and draw it through the first loop **(figure 23)**. Wrap the yarn anticlockwise once more, and draw it through both loops **(figure 24)**. Insert the hook into the next stitch **(figure 25)**. Wrap the yarn and draw it through the first loop, then wrap the yarn again and draw it through both loops. Continue in this manner.

■ **figure 22**

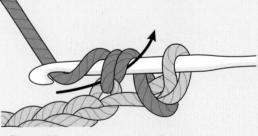

■ **figure 23**

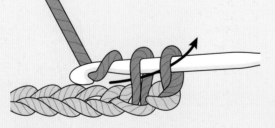

■ **figure 24**

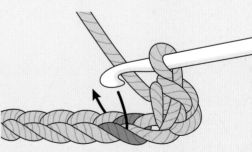

■ **figure 25**

ABBREVIATIONS

approx	approximately		**patt**	pattern
b	back		**p or P**	purl
beg	begin/beginning		**PM**	place marker
bet	between		**p2tog**	purl 2 stitches together
ch	chain		**p1 tbl**	purl 1 through back loop
cm	centimeter(s)			
cn	cable needle		**pwise**	purlwise
cont	continue		**rem**	remain/remaining
dc	double crochet		**rep**	repeat(s)
dec	decrease		**RH**	right hand
dpn(s)	double pointed needle(s)		**RS**	right side
			sc	single crochet
est	established		**sl**	slip
f	front		**SM**	slip marker
foll	follow(s)/following		**ssk**	slip, slip, knit these 2 stitches together
g	gram			
G st	Garter stitch		**st(s)**	stitch(es)
inc	increase/ increases/ increasing		**St st**	Stocking stitch
			tbl	through back loop
			tog	together
k or K	knit		**wyib**	with yarn in back
k1 tbl	knit 1 through back loop		**wyif**	with yarn in front
			WS	wrong side
kwise	knitwise		**yd(s)**	yard(s)
k2tog	knit 2 stitches together		**yf**	yarn forward (an increase)
LH	left hand			
m	meter(s)		**yo**	yarn over
mm	millimeter(s)			
M1	make 1 stitch			
oz	ounce(s)			

NEEDLE CONVERSION CHART

METRIC (MM)	U.S.	METRIC (MM)	U.S.
2	0	5.5	9
2.25	1	6	10
2.5	1	6.5	10½
2.75	2	7	10½
3	3	8	11
3.25	3	9	13
3.5	4	10	15
3.75	5	12	17
4	6	15	19
4.25	6	19	35
4.5	7	20	36
5	8	25	50

YARN WEIGHT CHART

YARN WEIGHT CATEGORIES	lace	fingering	sport	double knitting	aran	chunky	extra chunky
TYPE OF YARNS IN CATEGORY	Fingering, 10-count crochet thread	Sock, Fingering, Baby	Sport, Baby	DK, Light, Worsted	Worsted, Afghan, Aran	Chunky, Craft, Rug	Bulky, Roving

about the
designers

■ **COO** *page 10*
■ **IMPULSE** *page 18*
■ **TEASE** *page 24*

ELLA AVERBUKH is a New York-based knit apparel and accessories designer. She comes from a long line of crafters and considers knitting a form of art therapy. Ella believes knitters engage their artistic side when choosing different colors and textures of yarn, and that a great feeling of accomplishment comes upon project completion. Ella designs primarily for women; her knit art juxtaposes such seemingly opposing elements of the female psyche as vulnerability and power, and fragility and tenacity. She is inspired by various fashion periods, but her work mostly reflects Renaissance, Medieval, Victorian, and Art Nouveau aesthetics. She exhibits her designs in numerous international trade shows, and her work can be found in New York City and in European boutiques.

MARY JANE BARRY lives in Hamilton, Ontario, in Canada, where she works as a registered nurse with special-needs children. She also finds the time to make fiber art, and has a business creating and selling various hand-knit items of her own design. Mary

Jane grew up on the east coast of Canada in St. John, New Brunswick, in a large family of Irish heritage. There, she learned an appreciation for a slower pace of life, love of home and family, and the value of handmade items and the handmade culture as a whole. Mary Jane's work reflects her love of simple design and she often uses natural materials and colors. See more of her hand knitting at www.thenatureofmaryjane.etsy.com.

■ **CATCH** *page 70*

■ **ENCHANTING** *page 22*

SIOBHAN BROWN learned to knit when she was 30, and if she has any regrets in life, it's that she missed all those years that could have been spent knitting and obsessing over yarn. Four years later, she's a compulsive knitter living with an ever-increasing stash in a Liverpool house that's *way* to small to accommodate the monstrous hoard she intends to collect (a man and a cat also share the space). Designing knitwear was a natural progression for Siobhan; it derives from an impatience with traditional patterns and having too short an attention span to see those through before starting something that she's thought up. Find her at www.stitchology.com.

JOANNA BOXALL is a designer, maker, and knitter living in Kent, in the U.K. After graduating with a BA (Hons) in Textile Design, where she specialized in knits, Joanna started an online hand-knitted accessory company named Dolly Knits. She creates modern and on-trend accessories using high-quality yarns in a wide variety of colors. Joanna

■ **BLUSH** *page 96*

sells through a number of online craft websites and boutiques in London, England. Her website is www.dollyknits.com.

■ **FRIVOLOUS** *page 66*

JOLYNN BURT'S great-grandmother got her started knitting when she was seven, and she's been doing it ever since. Now a great-grandmother herself, she enjoys knitting for her seven grandchildren and her great-grandchild. Since she retired, Jolynn has even more time to knit—and she *loves* it.

ESTHER MYONG CHUNG is an indie designer in Columbus, Ohio. She's sewn and knitted since grade school and graduated from the School of the Art Institute of Chicago with a BFA focus in fashion. As a student, she received a Marshall Field's Emmanuel Ungaro Scholarship in 2002 and won the 2003 Styles Scotland Fashion design competition. One summer she interned with New York designer Gary Graham, who is also an independent designer, and decided she wanted to follow the same path. Esther prefers to design for the fall and winter and combines historical- and nature-inspired themes into a clean, modern style with comfort in mind. She takes custom orders regularly and has international customers as well as local ones. She also teaches several fashion classes at the Columbus College of Art and Design.

ROSARIO THURY CORNEJO lives, designs, and knits in Buenos Aires, Argentina. After studying industrial design and art at Buenos Aires University, she worked as an interior designer for 10 years. Rosario has always knitted as a hobby, designing things for herself. Over time, her love of

■ **GLANCES** *page 72*

yarns became stronger and she has now fully dedicated herself to it. Her independent brand is named oveja negra.

■ **WISH** *page 76*

CARRIE APPLE EDDLEMAN is a 30-something wife who gave up a successful career as a graphic designer to become a homemaker and mother of three, a decision she'll never regret. She loves to find new ways to be creative. Knitting is currently her fix, and she adores designing inventive wearable art. She lives in Oak Ridge, North Carolina, and has two online stores where she sells her creations: lilyandlulu.etsy.com, and theartfulapple.etsy.com.

Following an ill-advised and largely unsuccessful attempt in the early '80s to knit a scarf for her Cabbage Patch doll, **BETSY FARQUHAR** abandoned yarn until a strange argument with her college boyfriend inspired her to crochet an afghan. Crochet gave way to knitting, and regular knitting gave way to obsessive knitting. Her work is informed by digital images; she likes to think of

■ **WINK** *page 14*
■ **RAPT** *page 50*

each knitted stitch as a pixel. She lives with the recipient of the afore-mentioned afghan—now her husband—and a 24-pound cat in Schenectady, New York.

LEIGH-ANNE FREDERICK has been designing things for as long as she can remember. Her mother often recounts stories of a little Leigh-Anne creating toys for herself and her sister to play with. She was taught to crochet by her aunt at the tender age of six, and when she was eight, her grandmother taught her

■ **DIZZY** *page 98*

to knit. Right from the start, she created items for her dolls, for herself, and as gifts for others. At age 13, she sold her first piece—a custom order for a baby blanket. You could say she was hooked. To this day, her creative spirit often keeps her awake at night, plotting her next design or project. Leigh-Anne finally listened to the little voice in her head, and after lots of hard work turned her passion into her own company, named L.A. Originals, so she's now a full-time designer and fiber artist. View more of her original designs at laoriginals.etsy.com and knitrgal.etsy.com.

IRINA GRINEVITSKY designs jewelry and objects using wood, ceramics, and leather, but a special place in her heart is reserved for knitting design: it's a wonderful opportunity to play with the texture and color of yarn. Irina comes from a family with multifaceted artistic interests:

■ **TICKLE** *page 84*

her grandmother, an architect, was also interested in clothing design; a grandfather was a landscape architect and a sculptor; and her father loved creating jewelry from exotic wood. Irina's jewelry and accessories have been successfully selling in New York boutiques as well as internationally. She calls New York City home.

DIANA "THE CRAFTAHOLIC" GONZALEZ knits, crochets, blogs, plays with paper, and chases after her daughter in the wonderful city of Brooklyn, New York. She runs a craft group called The NYC Craft Circle, and has her work on Etsy. Besides the couture knitwear and accessories she sells at www.sweetbuddhaknits.com, you can find her carved stamps and unique paper goods at www.sweetbuddha.etsy.com. The popular blog Confessions of a Craftaholic (www.confessionsofacraftaholic.blogspot.com) is also her handiwork.

BRENDA LAVELL learned to knit in grade school, despite her not-very-patient grandmothers. Almost 30 years later, she was still knitting, mostly scarves for herself or made as gifts, and she decided to start a design-related business in addition to her career as a university administrator. She chose knitting over jewelry making because she thought

■ **FLIRT** *page 80*

it would be less expensive than feeding her bead addiction. Ironically, her current yarn inventory is too large to admit to in print! Brenda calls her style "rustic elegance"—she uses largely artisanal yarns and classic techniques to create accessories with clean and elegant lines. However, she loves working with any fiber that has beautiful texture and color. Brenda lives in the San Francisco Bay area; her original hand knits and knitting patterns are available online at phydeaux.etsy.com and she's known to frequent Ravelry when she has a spare minute (user name phydeaux).

Family lore has it that **ELIZABETH LOVICK** started to knit as a toddler: her Cornish grandmother got fed up with the tot leaning over the arm of her chair to watch her knit, so she gave the child wool and needles and told her to knit her own. Liz did... In school, Liz kept herself in clothes money by selling her aran sweaters to friends, and when bad health

■ **CAPTIVATING** *page 28*

forced her to stop teaching at the age of 40, she did what her forebears would have done: she turned to knitting again. Now, from her house on the shores of Scapa Flow in Orkney, Scotland, she designs and knits, specializing in designs that bring the patterns of the Northern Isles to a new audience. Most of the time, Liz has three projects going—one gansey sweater, one piece of lace, and one Fair Isle sweater—*and* ideas for future projects sketched out in her head and on paper. For relaxation she sticks to fiber, doing spinning and dyeing, and there's always a camera in her pocket. She knits with an audio book in the player and her two rescue Scotties at her feet, waiting for the next walk.

LINDA LUNN is a knitter, she just can't stop, and all her spare time—when not working, doing family stuff, and studying part time—is usually spent knitting, crafting, and reading about knitting and crafts. She blogs at http://queenofthefroggers. blogspot.com and sometimes sells

■ **BREATHLESS** *page 90*

things she's made on leafgreenhandmade.etsy.com...because friends and family really don't want any more of her handmade stuff!

SIMONE MEYER was born in Christchurch, New Zealand, in 1972 and lived there until December 1995. She then decided to do what many Kiwis do: the big O.E. (which means Overseas Experience). She spent two and a half years living in England, working crazy jobs to make money to fund her adventures. In early 1998, Simone's plan

■ **POUT** *page 86*

was to head back home with a stopover in Denver, Colorado. You know what they say about the best-laid plans. Simone met her husband while in Denver, and the rest, as they say, is history. Simone developed her love for knitting at an early age. For her business, Kiwi & Company, she designs a line of felted bags, cowls, collars, capelets, and lariats, and she's continuously developing new ideas. Simone is very proud of her line, and she personally hand knits all of her items with the highest quality materials. Visit her website at www.kiwiandcompany.com.

■ **WHISPER** *page 54*

AMY MICALLEF is a fiber artist based in Peachtree City, Georgia. Her work includes a wide range of items, including fashion knitting, wall hangings, toys, stuffed animals, jewelry, gifts, novelties, and even fabric-based replacement body parts. She enjoys working in many types of fiber art and crafts:

knitting, crochet, quilting, sewing, embroidery, cross-stitch, needle felting, and alterations. Her special talent: she can make *anything* from file folders and masking tape.

■ **CRUSH** *page 56*

TARA-LYNN MORRISON'S shop is small, but she has big aspirations as a self-taught knitter. She hopes to turn her passion for knitting and the creativity of her knit designing into a big future for her two children, her old man (an artist who contributes prints to the shop from time to time), and their cat. She loves to thrift shop for vintage treasures, watch films, read, and have beach picnics as often as possible, and she takes her knitting with her everywhere.

EWELINA OLESINSKA has had many professions—from nurse to teacher to hospital administration manager—but it seems she's recently rediscovered the most important one, designing and making fashion. Her mother taught her to knit as a little girl and it was great fun from the very beginning; she could finally

■ **GIDDY** *page 92*

make dresses for her dolls all on her own! For a long stretch of time, she knitted creations for family, friends, and herself, and even though it never occurred to her to go beyond that, there must have been a strong need to do so, because here she is doing it! Ewelina is of Polish origin, but currently resides in Canada with her fantastic husband and sweet baby daughter. Find her on Etsy shop, Evelda's Neverland, at www.eveldasneverland.etsy.com.

LANA O'NEILL grew up in Ukraine, in the city of Odessa, where she was surrounded by handmade objects created by her grandmothers. She learned how to crochet after receiving a book on making crocheted doll clothes for one birthday. Later, her mother showed her the knit and purl stitches, but back then she preferred crochet and made doilies

■ **SUGAR** *page 62*

in lacy colors for the uniforms of friends at school—her first steps toward having her own business. Deeper interest in knitting came during her first pregnancy. She just couldn't put the needles down. When people saw the things she had made for her son, they often asked her to make similar items for the kids in their families. That's how KnitBerry.com came into existence in October 2007. Lana knits, and sometimes crochets, children's clothing non-stop. It's a challenge to keep up with orders and with her family's needs, but she enjoys designing for KnitBerry and tries to find time whenever possible. The greatest reward comes when her little customers— the youngsters who wear her knitwear—don't want to remove their hats and sweaters because they like wearing them so much... which is the feedback she gets all the time from parents!

ANET (KNITTING-NETTY) SKILLIN lives and works in Asheville, North Carolina. Mine-Grammie Ricker taught Anet "knit-in-en" when she was a little girl. Equal thanks and credit belong to Cheryl Waters of Houston, Texas, for her unwavering support, help with pattern writing, and for knitting the longer version of the cowl shown in this book.

■ **SPELLBOUND** *page 49*

BETH TODD is a fiber artist, published designer, and needlework/fiber arts instructor who lives in the Atlanta, Georgia, area with her wonderfully patient and tolerant husband, Ron. Together, they've raised six wonderful children, including twins. When she's not riding her Harley-Davidson

■ **COQUETTE** *page 38*

Lowrider, playing Celtic harp and drum, or belly dancing for exercise, Beth can be found creating original knit, crochet, or other fiber arts designs, some of which can be found in her online shop, www.bethtoddcreatz.etsy.com. Other examples of her work can be seen on her website: www.bethtodddesigns.com.

JANNA MARIA VALLÉE is a second-year textile arts student at Vancouver's Capilano University. She has a special fascination with yarn and its many textures and colors. After launching Vancouver's online yarn directory, Vancouver Yarn (www. vancouveryarn.com), Janna made

■ **DREAMY** *page 60*

many connections in her local textiles community, which is what brought her to Capilano. Upon beginning the program in 2008, Janna won the entrance scholarship, which recognizes excellence in application portfolios. She gravitated to the arts that involve color theory and yarn, and she excels at weaving and design. Aside from school, Janna is an avid blogger and she documents everything she dyes, knits, weaves, and designs. She stays busy updating her website and Etsy shop on a daily basis; keep abreast of new projects at www.jannamaria.com. She also continues to build on her line of yarns and patterns. Janna's project for this book is stitched up in her own 100% merino yarn, named Colossal Cozy. This yarn is her more affordable cashmere alternative, and it's so soft that if you've never been able to wear wool, now's the time to try again.

TANYA WADE is a native of Florida. She learned to knit at age 13. Her first knitted garment was a scarf she proudly wore to a U2 concert, stitched up in the colors of the Irish flag, of course. After a long hiatus, she picked up the sticks in her thirties and continues to knit and crochet to this day. She's proud to say she hand knit the

■ **CHARM** *page 34*

garment she wore at her nuptials in a Las Vegas chapel. Tanya is inspired by cinema, music, and the juxtaposition of romantic and urban sensibilities. She's a former newspaper editor, yarn store purchasing manager, and champion on the quiz show Jeopardy!. She enjoys nothing as much as knitting and designing while listening to a good DVD commentary, preferably one for an obscure French film. Follow her exploits at tanyadiva. wordpress.com.

■ **SPELLBOUND** *page 46*

CHERYL WATERS learned to knit as a child from her mother. After her mother passed away, she picked up the needles again to keep her mother's Christmas stocking tradition alive. Like her friend Anet Skillin, Cheryl is obsessed with knitting and loves helping others learn to do it, too.

acknowledgments

A WARM thank you to all the incredibly talented designers in this book—if you hadn't shared your pretty, delicate, sassy, and altogether awesome creations, this book would never have come into being!

Photo director Dana Irwin and photographer Lynne Harty and her assistants worked their magic once again—what a team!—capturing the perfect vibe on film and shining the spotlight on the amazing projects. (That cute little dog on page 56—it belongs to Lynne. She's always willing to go the extra mile!) Our models made the projects look that much lovelier; and make-up artist E. Scott Thompson (and his assistants—one of them, Anna, is shown here fighting the wind with her hairspray!) made the models look even lovelier, if possible. Our gratitude, too, to all the local businesses for sharing their spaces during location shoots, and to Magnolia Beauregard's—the sweetest antique shop in Asheville, North Carolina—for the loan, over and over again, of some precious accessories.

Thanks to tech editor Rita Greenfeder and to proofreader Suzanne Tourtillott for getting everything ship-shape; to Orrin Lundgren for his spot-on illustrations; and to the editorial team, especially Kathleen McCafferty, who worked on all aspects of this book. Pamela Norman pulled it all together with her delightful book design, while production assistant Bradley Norris didn't drop a stitch. We salute you with our knitting needles, cheer you with cups of chai, and wrap you up in heaps of thanks.

index